GUYANDOTTE JUV_NONFIC
616.99419 H
Harmon, Daniel E.
Leukemia :

DISCARD

CANCER AND MODERN SCIENCE™

LEUKEMIA

Current and Emerging Trends in Detection and Treatment

DANIEL E. HARMON

ROSEN PUBLISHING
New York

Published in 2012 by The Rosen Publishing Group, Inc.
29 East 21st Street, New York, NY 10010

Copyright © 2012 by The Rosen Publishing Group, Inc.

First Edition

All rights reserved. No part of this book may be reproduced in any form without permission in writing from the publisher, except by a reviewer.

Library of Congress Cataloging-in-Publication Data

Harmon, Daniel E.
Leukemia: current and emerging trends in detection and treatment / Daniel E. Harmon.—1st ed.
  p. cm.—(Cancer and modern science)
Includes bibliographical references and index.
ISBN 978-1-4488-1311-7 (library binding)
1. Leukemia—Juvenile literature. I. Title.
RC643.H2915 2012
616.99'419—dc22

2010015459

Manufactured in the United States of America

CPSIA Compliance Information: Batch #S11YA: For further information, contact Rosen Publishing, New York, New York, at 1-800-237-9932.

On the cover: A leukemia cell, which has been colored, is seen through a scanning electron microscope. Leukemia is a disease of the blood and lymph system.

CONTENTS

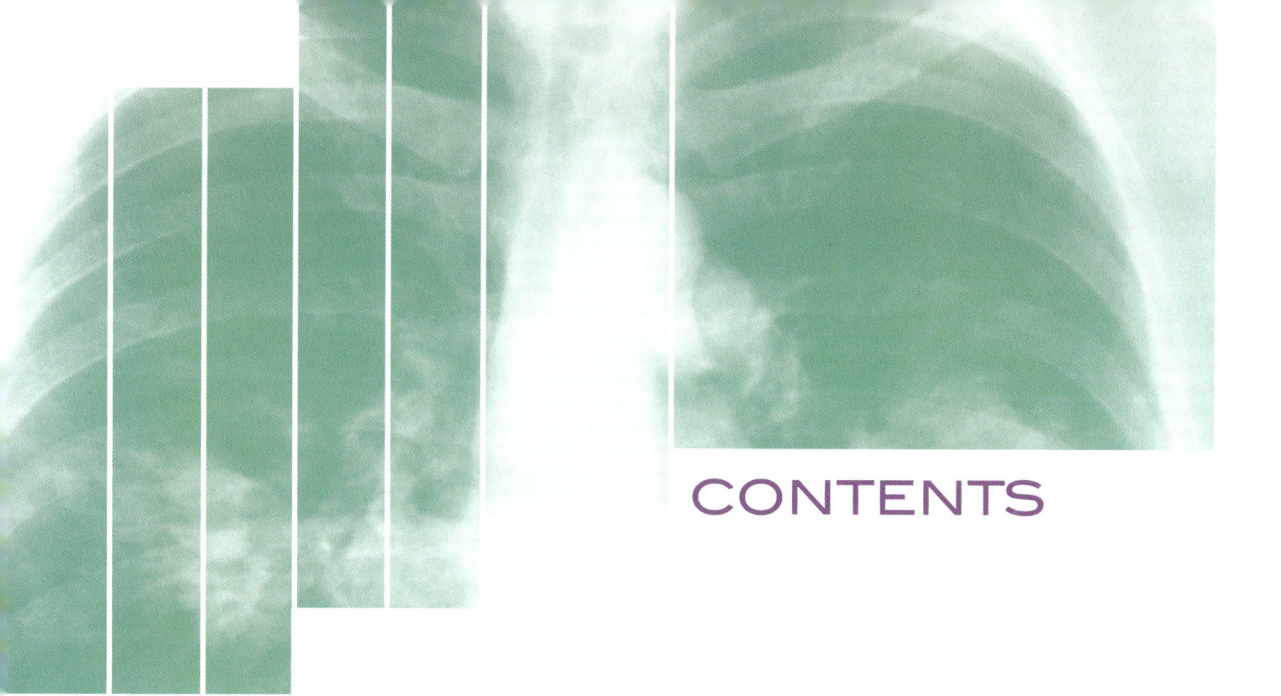

　　　　　　　　INTRODUCTION 4
CHAPTER 1　WHAT IS LEUKEMIA? 7
CHAPTER 2　POSSIBLE CAUSES OF LEUKEMIA 16
CHAPTER 3　TYPES OF LEUKEMIA 23
CHAPTER 4　SYMPTOMS, DIAGNOSIS, AND
　　　　　　　　ADVANCED STAGES 31
CHAPTER 5　TREATING AND COPING WITH
　　　　　　　　THE DISEASE 40
CHAPTER 6　STRATEGIES IN
　　　　　　　　LEUKEMIA RESEARCH 47
　　　　　　　　GLOSSARY 54
　　　　　　　　FOR MORE INFORMATION 56
　　　　　　　　FOR FURTHER READING 59
　　　　　　　　BIBLIOGRAPHY 60
　　　　　　　　INDEX 62

INTRODUCTION

Marie Curie (1867–1934) was a French scientist. She won two Nobel Prizes for the research that she and her husband, Pierre, performed. They studied radioactivity. Curie's later work led to major advances in science and medicine. In particular, it helped introduce radiation therapy for treating cancer patients.

Radiation, like many forms of medical treatment, can be very dangerous. In Curie's time, its dangers were not fully understood. She used to carry small containers of radioactive substances in her pockets. The radioactivity was likely absorbed at high levels into her body over many years. Even today, radiation traces can be detected on some of her laboratory notebooks. Most biographers attribute her close contact with radiation as the cause of her death: leukemia.

Her daughter, Irène Joliot-Curie (1897–1956), was also a noted scientist. She worked with her mother for many years and was regularly exposed to radiation. She, too, died of leukemia.

Leukemia, or cancer of the white blood cells, is generally fatal unless it is treated promptly. The Leukemia & Lymphoma Society estimates

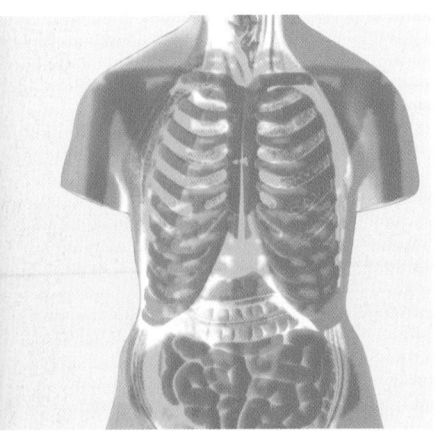

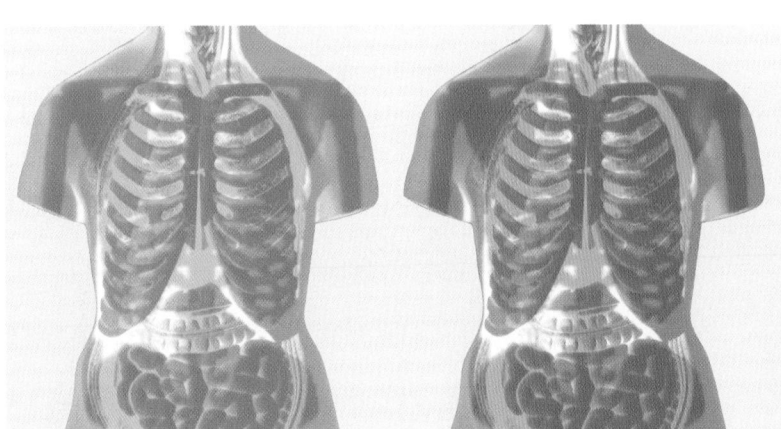

Chemist Marie Curie devoted her life to the study of radiation, helping to lead to the development of radiation therapy. Regular exposure to radiation is believed to have caused her death from leukemia.

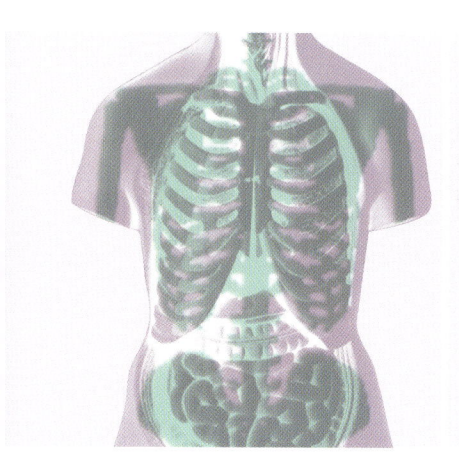

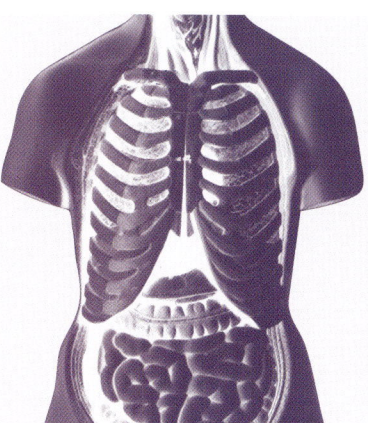

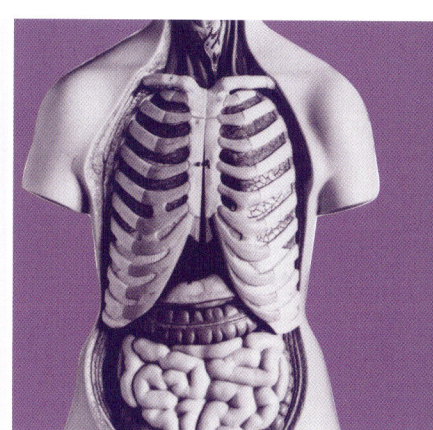

5

that one-quarter of a million Americans currently have or have had leukemia. Some 45,000 new cases of leukemia in adults and 3,500 cases in children are diagnosed annually in the United States. About 22,000 deaths in the United States are attributed to leukemia.

Thanks to the dedication of researchers like the Curies, leukemia has become more treatable, even curable, in most cases (although complete cure is never assured). Such research is actively continuing in the twenty-first century. Scientists are especially interested in the genetic changes (changes in the DNA and RNA) of white blood cells that lead to leukemia. They are also studying ways to improve treatments for patients with leukemia.

Although many advances have been made, there is still a long way to go. Medical scientists constantly seek ways to prevent and combat all forms of leukemia. Meanwhile, doctors, therapists, counselors, and other caregivers strive to provide patients with the best possible quality of life while they cope with the disease.

CHAPTER 1

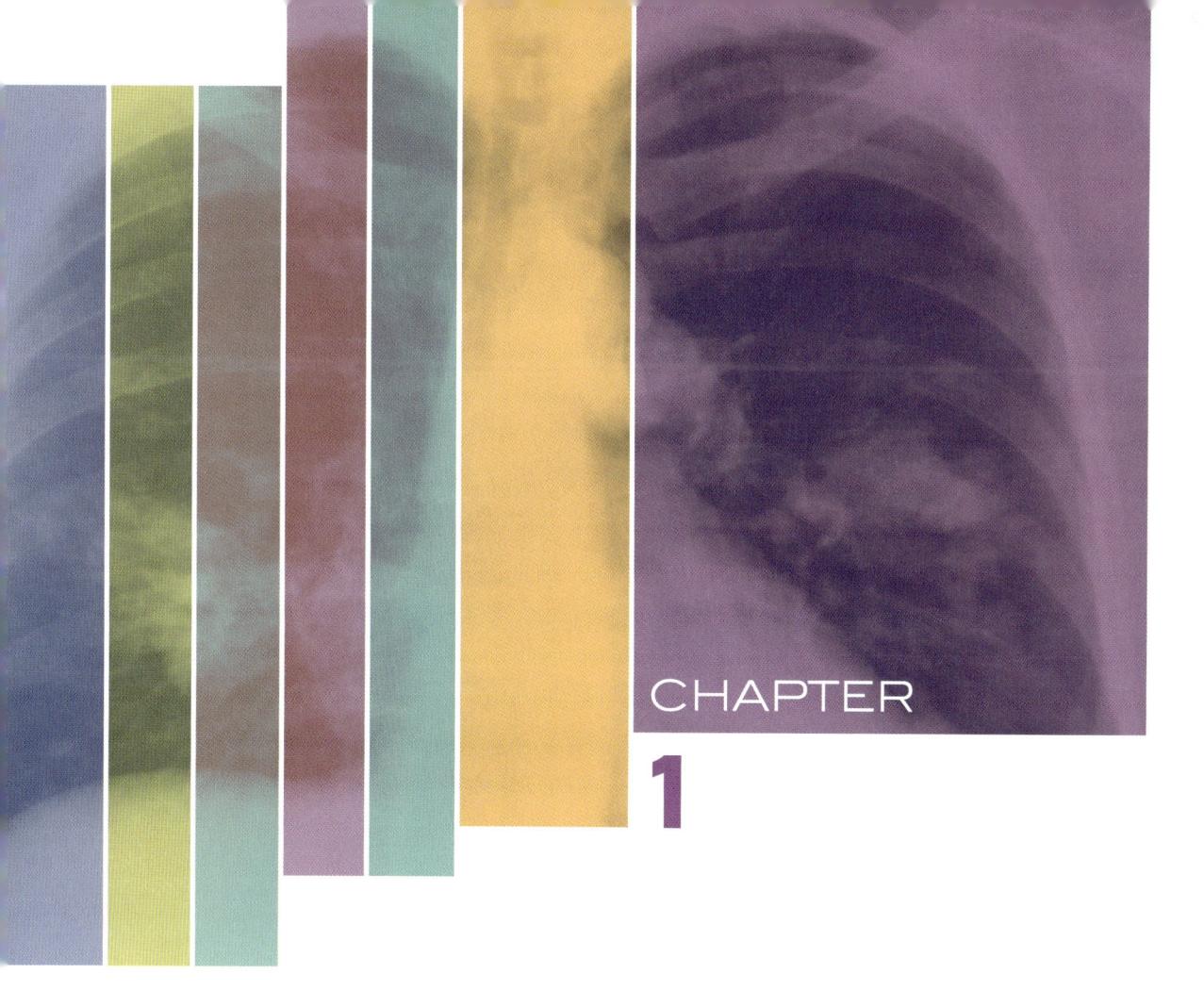

WHAT IS LEUKEMIA?

Dr. Bernadine Healy echoes other doctors in describing leukemia as "a disease of our DNA." In her book *Living Time*, she explains, "Cancer directly changes the DNA code, thereby altering the cell's fundamental identity and behavior and forever changing its future."

DNA is what defines the chemical makeup of a person's body. Each person's DNA is unique. Sometimes, our DNA can be damaged by various exposures, such as excessive sunlight or certain chemicals, or by random mutations (genetic changes). Our bodies are programmed to fix this damage. When DNA damage cannot be fixed, cancer can result.

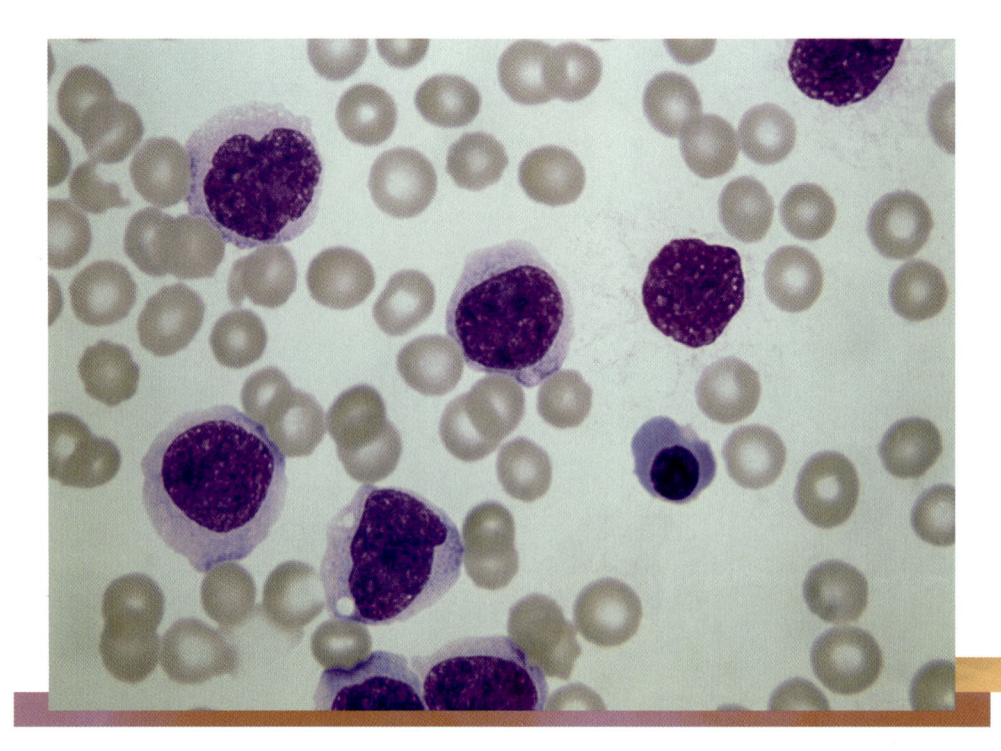

Immature white blood cells grow out of control inside the body of a leukemia patient. Leukemic cells take over the bone marrow and enter the bloodstream and lymph system.

Some people also inherit genetic changes from their family that predispose them to certain cancers.

Leukemia is what doctors call a liquid cancer. Liquid cancers develop from cells in the bone marrow and bloodstream and in the lymphatic system. They are different from solid cancers, which affect the skin, organs, and ducts. Just as there are many different kinds of white blood cells in our bone marrow, blood, and lymphatic systems, there are many different kinds of leukemias. Subtypes of leukemias are named for the white blood cells from which they develop. They are generally divided into lymphoid and myeloid categories. Leukemias can be acute (primitive and quickly growing) or chronic (more developed and slowly growing). The most common forms of leukemia in the United States are acute myelogenous leukemia (AML) and chronic lymphocytic leukemia (CLL).

According to the *Leukemia Sourcebook*, leukemia actually is "not a single disease, but a group of malignancies in which the bone marrow and blood-forming organs produce excessive numbers of white blood cells."

Fighting for Control of the Blood

Blood cells are created in a person's bone marrow. The bone marrow has been likened to the body's "blood factory." Bones are not solid but actually hollow. The hollow inner length of a living bone is filled with a soft pulp, called marrow. The bone marrow makes up as much as 5 percent of a person's body weight. It produces all of the blood cells that eventually escape to the blood vessels. Blood cells carry oxygen to the body's tissues, help fight infections, and make scabs to clot the blood when an injury occurs. Cells, like all life-forms, develop and grow. They also divide and multiply. Leukemia occurs when white blood cells develop genetic changes that allow them to grow out of control and escape the body's normal checks and balances. Over time, leukemic cells can fill the bone marrow and then spill out into the bloodstream and lymphatic vessels. Leukemic cells can also get stuck in various organs in the body, such as the spleen, liver, kidneys, lungs, and brain.

Patients with leukemia are often diagnosed when they experience unusual or excessive blood-related symptoms, such as unexplained bruising or extreme fatigue. Because the bone marrow gets crowded with leukemia cells, there is no room for many other healthy blood cells to live. The symptoms of leukemia will be discussed in more detail in chapter 4.

10 LEUKEMIA

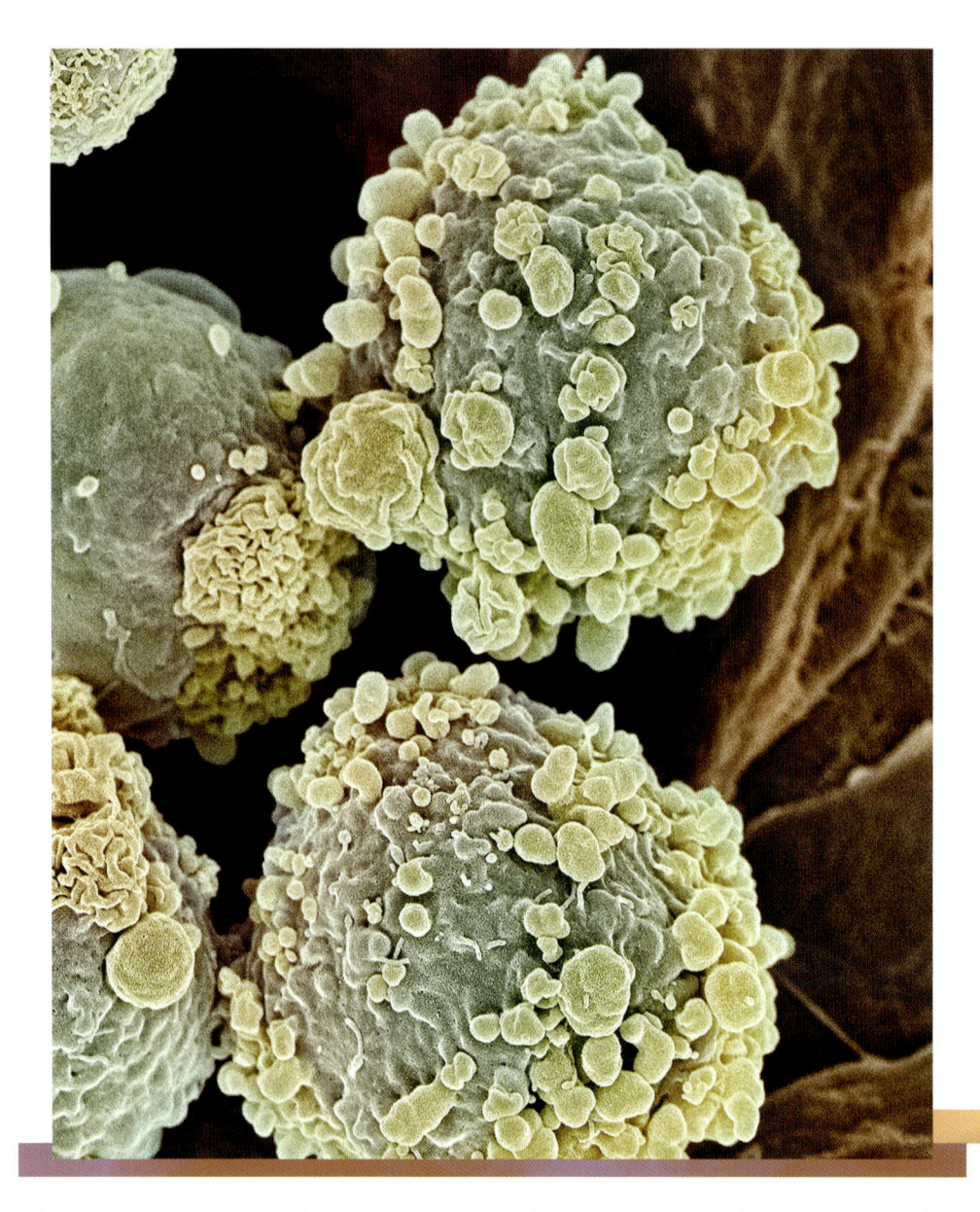

This sample of white cells was taken from the bloodstream of a chronic lymphocytic leukemia (CLL) patient.

History of the Disease

Leukemia and a similar blood disorder, lymphoma, have been killers for thousands of years. Cancer is thought to have existed since the beginning of human history. (It has existed in other life-forms as well.) Not until about 150 years ago, though, did doctors and scientists begin to understand the true nature of leukemias and lymphomas.

Until that time, doctors assumed that cancers and blood diseases were caused by abnormal amounts of certain fluids, called humors, in the body. Some of the treatments they gave patients were strange, ineffective, and more than a little scary. For instance, they often pierced the skin and let the blood flow freely. In this way, they thought they were draining undesirable substances from the body. In ancient Egypt and India, doctors made a paste of arsenic to apply to skin cancers. (Arsenic, used incorrectly, can be deadly. Throughout history, criminals have used it as a poison. But it can also be beneficial. Arsenic is used today to treat a certain type of leukemia.)

In the mid-1800s, European scientists and doctors began to suspect the true sources of cancer: the body's cells. Cancer research pioneers of the period included two Germans, Rudolf Virchow and Wilhelm Waldeyer. They linked cancer to corrupted cells that spread. Virchow proved that harmful cells originate in healthy body tissue. Waldeyer described how breast cancer develops and spreads to other parts of the body through the bloodstream and lymph system.

Another important German researcher was Ernst Neumann. He made vital discoveries in hematology, the study of blood cells. Among other findings, he demonstrated that red blood cells and white blood cells are produced in the bone marrow.

Leukemia, as it is now classified, was not initially identified as a cancer. In the mid-1800s, several doctors, including Virchow and Scottish pathologist

Rudolf Virchow, a German pathologist, was a researcher in the nineteenth-century who helped link cancer to damaged blood cells.

John Hughes Bennett, noted cases of patients who, at death, had extraordinarily enlarged spleens. They found in the dead patients' blood what they first thought was pus. Soon, the pus-like white substance in such cases was recognized as excessive levels of white blood cells. In time, doctors realized that the abnormal white blood cells represented no simple blood disease. They were cancer.

Research into this liquid form of cancer began. Effective treatments were not developed until the mid-twentieth century, however. Great advances in leukemia research have been made in the past fifty years, which has improved cure rates and survival for patients with leukemia.

Leukemia Statistics

The Leukemia & Lymphoma Society reports that almost a quarter of a million Americans currently have leukemia. For some, the disease is in remission, and they lead almost normal lives. Others are struggling to survive.

LEUKEMIA GETS ITS NAME

Rudolf Virchow (1821–1902) was one of the leading doctors and medical researchers of the nineteenth century. Born in what is now Poland, he was educated in Berlin, Germany, where he conducted most of his work. Virchow was a pathologist, a doctor who examines the effects of diseases on the body. He was only twenty-nine years old when he wrote his classic medical work on cellular pathology. At the time, most doctors assumed that diseases are born in the body's organs or tissues. Virchow believed they originate at the microscopic level—in cells. Because of his important research, Virchow is considered the founder of modern cellular pathology.

Among his contributions was his study of the then-mysterious disease that is now called leukemia. Virchow first labeled the disease *weisse Blut*, German for "white blood." It became better known by the Greek version. The Greek prefix *leuk-* (or *leuko-*) means "pale" or "white." *Haima* is Greek for "blood."

For the most part, leukemia is a disease of older people. Ten times as many adults acquire leukemia than children under the age of fifteen. The median age of new patients with leukemia is sixty-six years. Some twenty-two thousand Americans die of leukemia every year. Leukemia is the fifth-deadliest cancer form in men and the seventh deadliest in women in the United States. AML is one of the deadliest types. More than 90 percent of new AML cases are diagnosed in adults.

There are encouraging statistics, though. For instance, advances in childhood leukemia treatments during the past forty years have drastically reduced the death rate from leukemia among children under the

This teen leukemia survivor in North Carolina organized Pediatric Cancer Awareness Day as an Eagle Scout project to benefit a children's hospital.

age of fifteen. Success rates are especially good for children with acute lymphocytic leukemia (ALL), a fast-developing cancer that is quickly fatal if untreated. Of the 3,500 cases of childhood leukemia in the United States each year, fewer than 500 of these children will die as a result of leukemia.

Still, leukemia remains a serious, often fatal, health threat. The likelihood of treatment success depends on the type of leukemia, the genetic changes that have occurred, the patient's age, and the patient's response to treatment. Researchers are working to find more effective therapies and, if possible, develop preventive measures. The problem in prevention research, however, is that the causes of leukemia are not entirely understood.

MYTHS AND FACTS

MYTH Getting diagnosed with leukemia is like getting a death sentence.

FACT Just fifty years ago, the chance of surviving leukemia was slim. With scientific and medical advances through the years, though, many people with leukemia can now be successfully treated. The cure rates for childhood leukemia are particularly good. Survival statistics mainly depend on the type of leukemia and the patient's age at diagnosis.

MYTH Leukemia is more common in children than adults.

FACT Cancer is the most common disease-related cause of death in children fourteen years old and younger. Leukemia is the most common cancer of childhood, with approximately 3,500 new diagnoses each year in the United States. Nonetheless, leukemia remains more common in adults, with more than 45,000 new cases diagnosed each year.

MYTH Leukemia can be caused by coming close to electrical power lines.

FACT Some doctors and researchers in the past suspected a link between leukemia and exposure to high levels of electrical current. Various studies have been conducted, but results remain inconclusive. At this time, few environmental exposures have been linked definitively to causing leukemia.

CHAPTER 2

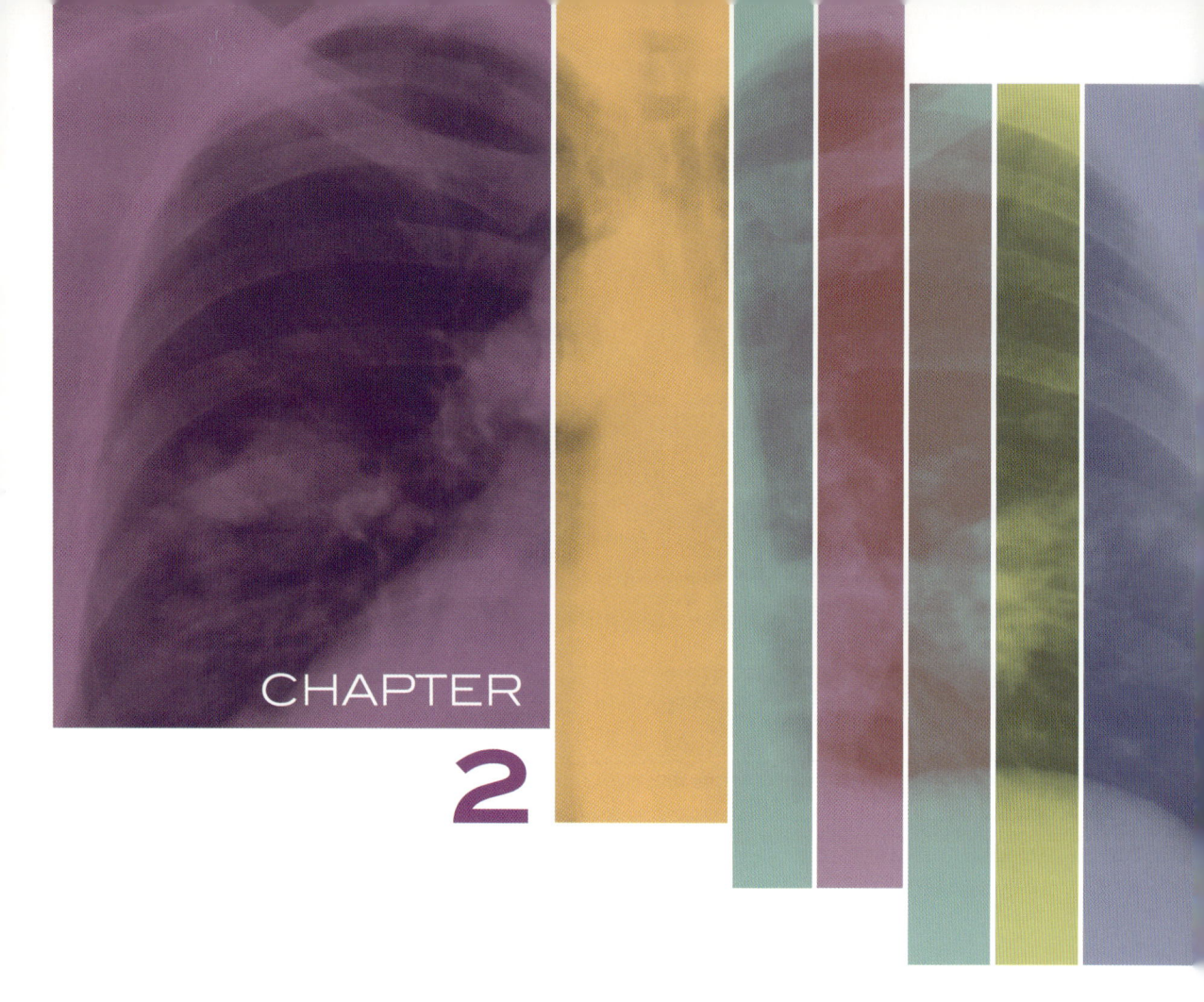

POSSIBLE CAUSES OF LEUKEMIA

In most cases, the cause of leukemia is a mystery. A variety of factors are believed to play a role, and research is actively ongoing to figure out these links. Potential factors include exposure to high-energy radiation, pesticides and herbicides, and other chemicals. Certain viruses may be linked to one kind of leukemia.

Researchers know only that such factors might put a person at greater risk for acquiring leukemia. Proof is difficult. Some people who are regularly exposed to certain pesticides, for example, have developed

Researchers like Robert Charles Gallo (second from left) *at the National Cancer Institute and elsewhere work to learn more about cancer causes and possible cures.*

leukemia; others with even greater exposure to the same chemicals have not gotten sick.

Possible Contributing Factors

Countless studies have suggested possible causes or contributors to leukemia. Here are some of the leading suspects.

Viruses. Certain viruses can cause deadly diseases. The most infamous example in modern times is the connection between the human immunodeficiency virus (HIV) and acquired immunodeficiency syndrome (AIDS). During the 1970s, Robert Gallo, a virologist, discovered a link between a virus classified as human T-lymphotropic virus type I (HTLV-I) and a form of leukemia. Like HIV, HTLV-I can be transmitted between humans by blood transfusions, sexual activity, and breastfeeding. HTLV-I infection can cause a rare form of cancer called adult T-cell leukemia/lymphoma.

Radiation. Most historians assume that radiation caused the leukemias of Marie Curie and her daughter. Both scientists were exposed to excessive radiation during their research studies. Excessive radiation is dangerous because it can cause unhealthy changes in cells. Extreme examples of excessive radiation exposure are nuclear accidents and explosions. Hiroshima and Nagasaki in Japan were the scenes of atomic bomb devastation at the end of World War II (1939–1945). For years afterward, thousands of Japanese who lived near those cities developed horrible diseases like leukemia. Unfortunately, leukemia and other diseases have sometimes been linked to radiation therapy—the standard doses used to treat cancer patients.

Exposure to chemicals. Besides pesticides and herbicides, benzene has been identified as a cause of leukemia. Occasional exposure is not a concern, but constant exposure over a long period of time is. Benzene is used in making solvents, glue, and other household products. It is also contained in unleaded gasoline. Other common consumer products, including hair dyes, have been mentioned—but not proved—as potential culprits.

As with radiation therapy, some chemotherapy medicines can also cause later leukemias (secondary leukemias). Doctors know that cancer patients who have received larger doses of certain chemotherapies are at a slightly higher risk for developing secondary leukemia, particularly acute myelogenous leukemia (AML). Without chemotherapy and radiation, though, people would likely die of their cancers.

Electromagnetic fields. For years, some researchers have suspected that close contact with power lines and other electromagnetic fields—possibly including household electrical appliances—is a potential cause of leukemia. High levels of current, like radiation, can alter a person's cell structure.

Smoking. Studies have suggested a possible link between smoking and various forms of cancer, including myelogenous leukemias.

Genetics. Researchers have found little evidence to link family history to leukemia,

A teenager with Down syndrome works at a computer. Scientists believe conditions such as Down syndrome may increase the likelihood of a person developing leukemia.

although a sibling of a patient with leukemia is at a slightly higher risk for developing leukemia. Certain genetic diseases can place an individual at greater risk for getting leukemia. An example is Down syndrome, a condition that causes physical problems and learning disabilities. This possible link has been noticed especially in cases of acute lymphocytic leukemia (ALL) among children. Other genetic syndromes, such as Noonan syndrome, have been linked to an increased risk of AML.

Advancing age. As people grow older, they are more at risk for abnormal cells to develop. *The Mayo Clinic Family Health Book* points out that more than half of leukemia cases are diagnosed in people older than sixty.

WHAT IS HAPPENING IN THE BONE MARROW?

Whatever the cause, the effect of leukemia is a change in the makeup of the blood. As explained in chapter 1, leukemia begins its campaign to conquer the human body by building an army—an army of bad blood cells. Once they form, the bad cells multiply and crowd out the good cells.

White blood cells work to prevent infections. Red blood cells (which give blood its color) distribute oxygen throughout the body and carry away poisonous carbon dioxide. Both red blood cells and white blood cells are formed in the bone marrow. The bone marrow also produces platelets, which enable blood to clot when a skin cut or internal injury occurs.

With leukemia, the bad white blood cells interfere with the balance of other cells' production inside the bone marrow. Leukemia cells crowd out normal, functional white blood cells. This process lowers the body's resistance to disease and ability to fight infections. Leukemia cells also disrupt the normal production of red blood cells and platelets. Such disruption can lead to anemia (low levels of red blood cells) and problems with excessive bruising and bleeding. Even slight cuts and bruises become serious because normal blood clotting does not occur. The likelihood of infection increases.

Can Leukemia Be Prevented?

If researchers can pinpoint the causes of a disease, they have gone a long way toward finding ways to treat it and perhaps even prevent it. Because the causes of leukemia have not been identified for certain, no preventative measures are currently known.

The best prevention of diseases is to stay as healthy as possible. Substance abuse—smoking and the abuse of alcohol and other risky drugs—has been linked to cancer and other dangerous illnesses. So has obesity. A sensible diet (more fiber, less fat) and regular exercise support an effective natural immune system.

Otherwise, statistics indicate that lifestyles generally do not affect the occurrence of leukemia. Social, racial, and economic factors are not thought to play a major role, but such factors may be implicated in certain leukemia types. Interestingly, one form of the disease, acute lymphocytic leukemia, is found to be more common in wealthier or privileged societies. Another type, chronic lymphocytic leukemia, is more likely to occur in people of European ancestry than in Asian populations.

Although no specific foods or diet supplements are known to prevent leukemia, doctors point out that a healthy lifestyle, including eating cereal high in fiber, is the most effective deterrent to diseases.

Still, scientists are not sure which characteristics of societies place those people at greater or less risk.

On its Leukemia Facts & Statistics Web site, the Leukemia & Lymphoma Society summarizes, "Anyone can get leukemia. Leukemia affects males and females of all ages. The cause of leukemia is not known."

CHAPTER
3

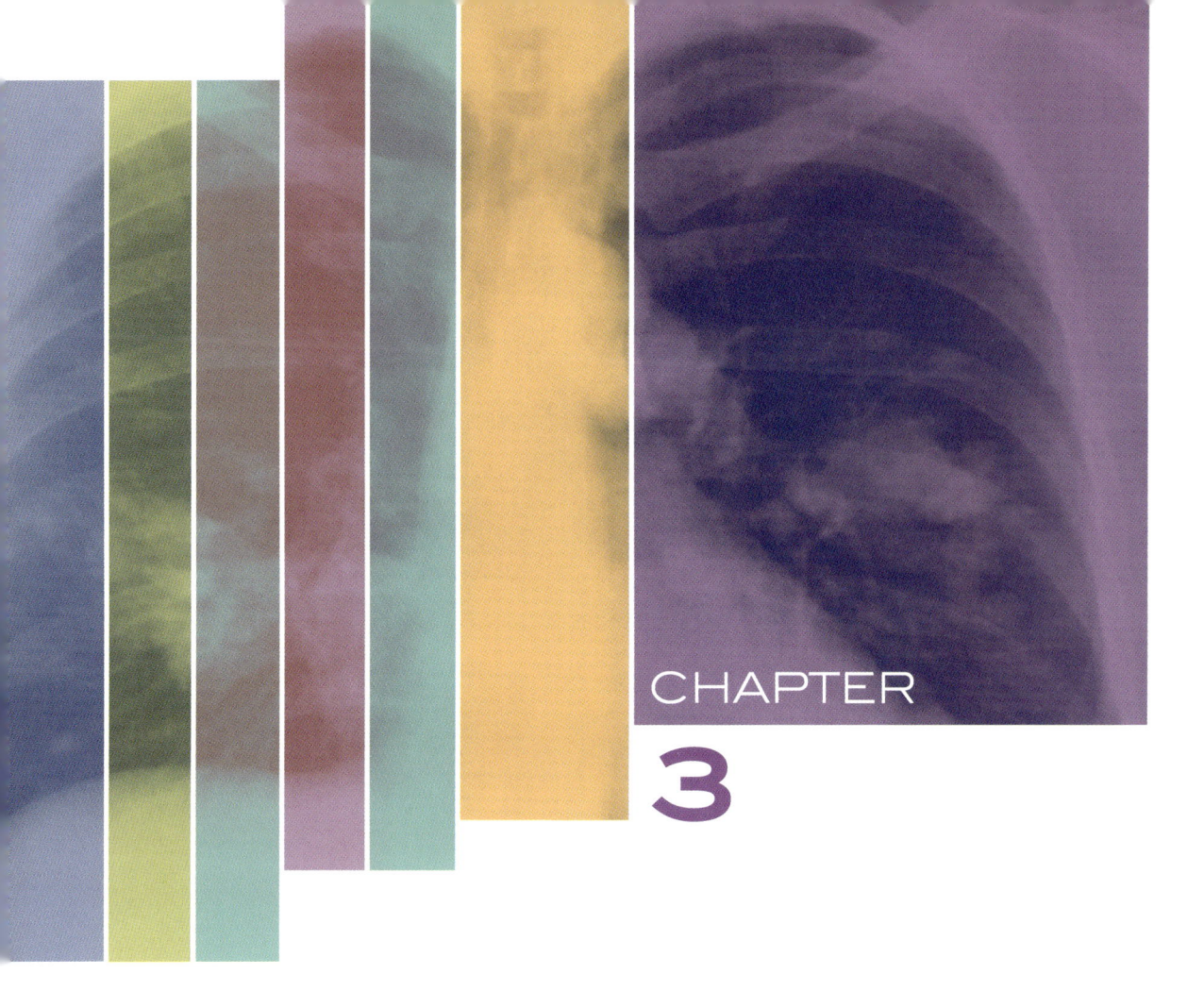

TYPES OF LEUKEMIA

Leukemia is a malignant disease of the white blood cells, and it can spread anywhere in the body. Leukemia starts in a person's bone marrow—the "blood factory" where blood cells are produced. As the bone marrow fills with leukemia, the bad cells can overflow, spill out into the bloodstream, and travel throughout the body.

In general, there are two types of leukemia: acute and chronic. Acute leukemias develop rapidly from early, immature white blood cells. Chronic types develop more slowly from cells at later stages of

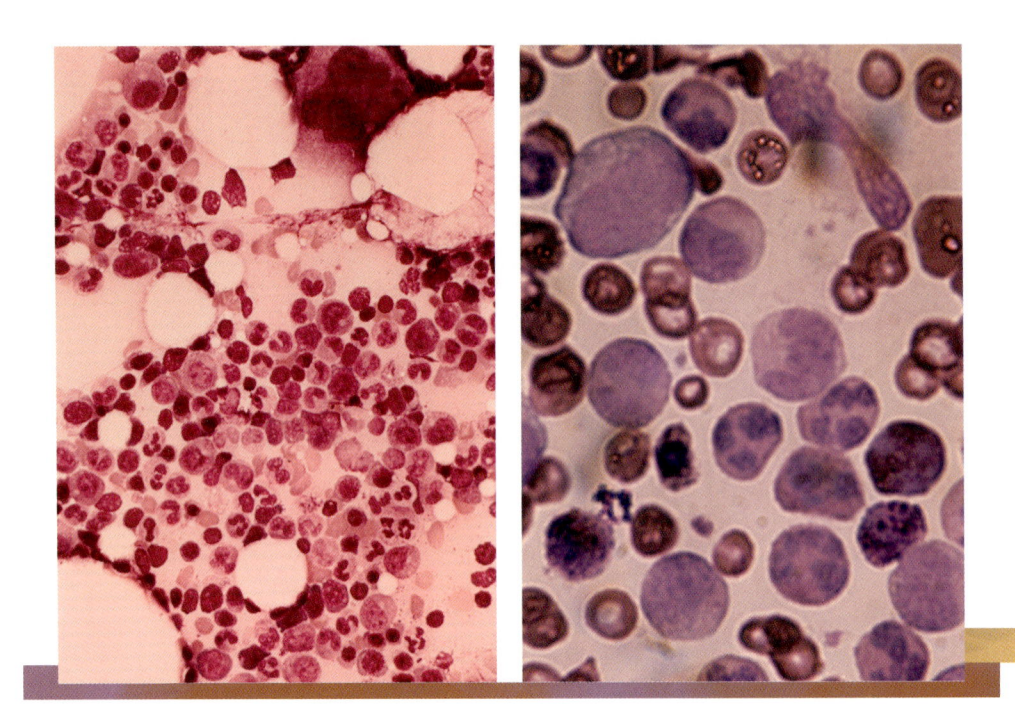

These images show acute (left) and chronic (right) forms of leukemia. Leukemia cells spread from the bone marrow and bloodstream throughout the body.

development. Acute leukemia types, if not diagnosed and treated quickly, are usually fatal—often within weeks to months. Because of slower development, chronic leukemia forms are routinely misdiagnosed as less serious diseases. They may not be diagnosed as leukemia and properly treated until they have reached a serious stage. If they are recognized early in their development, they can be treated successfully in most cases.

In addition to acute and chronic forms, leukemias are categorized by the types of cells from which they arise. The two major categories are lymphocytic (developing from lymphocytes) and myelogenous (developing from myeloid cells). The four major types of leukemia are thus acute lymphocytic leukemia (ALL), chronic lymphocytic leukemia (CLL), acute myelogenous leukemia (AML), and chronic myelogenous leukemia (CML).

Acute lymphocytic leukemia (ALL) may also be known as acute lymphoblastic leukemia. It is the most common cancer that occurs in children and accounts for about 80 percent of all childhood leukemias. Certain genetic changes in ALL are associated with good cure rates, while other genetic changes tend to result in bad outcomes, like treatment resistance and relapse (recurrence of leukemia). Research and treatment advances have dramatically increased cure rates for childhood ALL over the past several decades. ALL accounts for only 10 to 20 percent of adult leukemias and is much harder to treat in adults than in children.

Chronic lymphocytic leukemia (CLL) is a slow form of leukemia that mainly occurs in older adults. Abnormal white blood cells develop and multiply, but this process takes place much more slowly than in acute leukemias. Some victims survive CLL for years without treatment. In many cases, doctors who diagnose the disease do not even recommend initial chemotherapy for CLL because studies indicate that early treatment does not improve the long-term survival rates of CLL patients. Besides, the side effects and possible complications of treatment can be worse than the leukemia itself. According to *The Mayo Clinic Family Health Book*, a third of CLL patients continue to lead normal lives even without treatment. However, if the disease progresses, chemotherapy and other forms of treatment, such as a bone marrow transplant, may be necessary.

26 LEUKEMIA

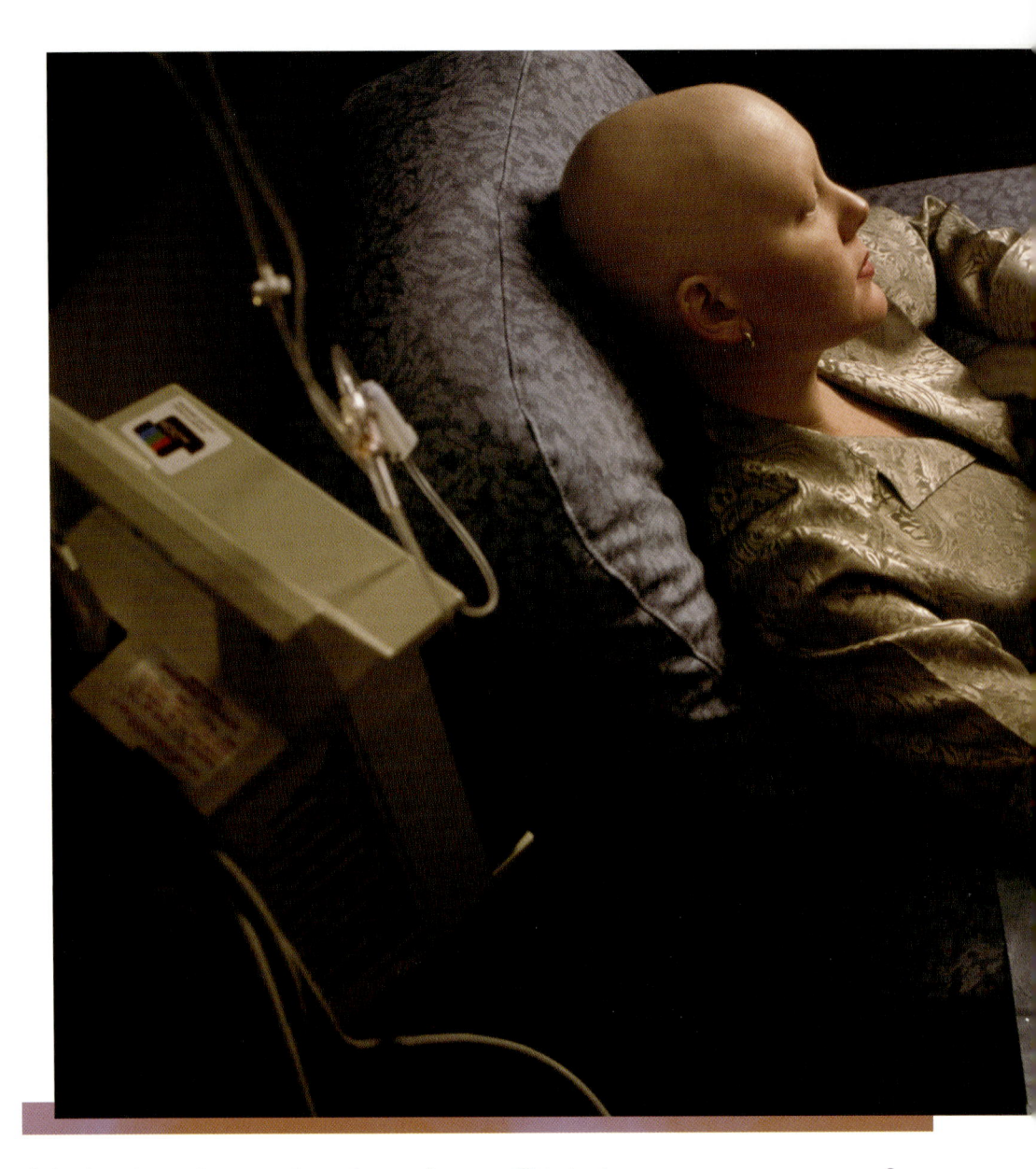

A leukemia patient receives chemotherapy. This is the most common type of treatment for patients with systemic diseases such as liquid cancers.

TYPES OF LEUKEMIA 27

Acute myelogenous leukemia (AML) develops from young myeloid cells and accounts for the majority of adult leukemias and a minority of childhood leukemias. There are many subtypes of AML; some are more common than others. Like ALL, AML must be diagnosed and treated promptly, or it can be rapidly fatal. Characteristic genetic changes in this group of leukemias also predict whether a patient with AML will be cured. AML is treated with intensive chemotherapy and often with a bone marrow transplant.

Chronic myelogenous leukemia (CML) is a less common form of leukemia that occurs primarily in adults, rarely in children. CML is caused by a unique genetic change where two chromosomes (that contain the cells' DNA) swap parts. This genetic change results in the "Philadelphia chromosome" (so named because it was discovered during tests conducted in Philadelphia, Pennsylvania). Although considered a chronic leukemia, most cases of CML eventually transform into acute leukemia and require aggressive treatment.

INTERESTING FACTS ABOUT LEUKEMIA

The Leukemia & Lymphoma Society reports many intriguing findings about different forms of leukemia. Here are some examples:

- The most common cancer in children who are one to seven years old is acute lymphocytic leukemia (ALL). Some six thousand new cases are diagnosed annually around the world. About 1,500 deaths from ALL occur each year. ALL causes more deaths among fifteen- to nineteen-year-olds than any other disease.

- An estimated 57 percent of new leukemia cases occur among males.

- Chronic lymphocytic leukemia (CLL) and acute myelogenous leukemia (AML) are the most common leukemia types found in adults. Some 9,000 deaths occur annually because of AML, while approximately 4,300 deaths result from CLL. Chronic myelogenous leukemia (CML) accounts for about five hundred annual deaths, on average.

- Chronic leukemia types (CLL and CML) account for 11 percent more reported cases than acute leukemias (ALL and AML).

Although the death rate among children with leukemia has plummeted in the last forty years, the society points out that "leukemia causes more deaths than any other cancer among children and young adults under age twenty."

Besides the four main forms of leukemia, rare subtypes occur. Hairy cell leukemia is a variation of CLL. It occurs only in older individuals, not in children and adolescents. It gets its name from the hairy appearance of the leukemia cells under a microscope lens. Hairy cell leukemias tend to affect the spleen in particular and may result in the rupture of the spleen if it gets too full of leukemia. Like other leukemias, the cause of hairy cell leukemia remains unknown.

Blood Tests Identify the Perpetrator

If a doctor is worried about a person having leukemia, a checkup and initial blood tests are the first steps in making the diagnosis. Later tests will likely include bone marrow testing. Through a process called aspiration,

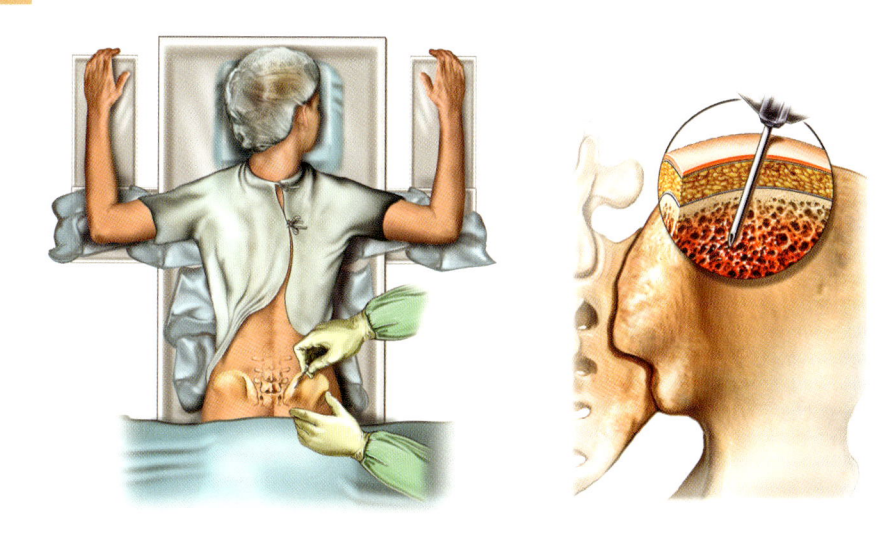

Bone marrow aspiration involves extracting a marrow sample from a hip bone. A medical technician looks for the presence of abnormal cells in the sample.

doctors remove a small amount of liquid bone marrow. In a biopsy, they also remove a small sliver of bone marrow. These samples are examined under a microscope.

A spinal tap will likely be performed for patients with acute leukemias. In this procedure, doctors draw a small sample of cerebrospinal fluid from the lower spine. This clear fluid around the spinal cord and brain serves as natural protection. By examining its color and makeup, analysts can determine if the leukemia has spread to these vital areas of the body.

Specialized testing of the bone marrow and spinal fluid will determine whether the disease is leukemia or a different blood disorder. If it is leukemia, the tests will reveal what type it is and indicate how best to treat it.

CHAPTER 4

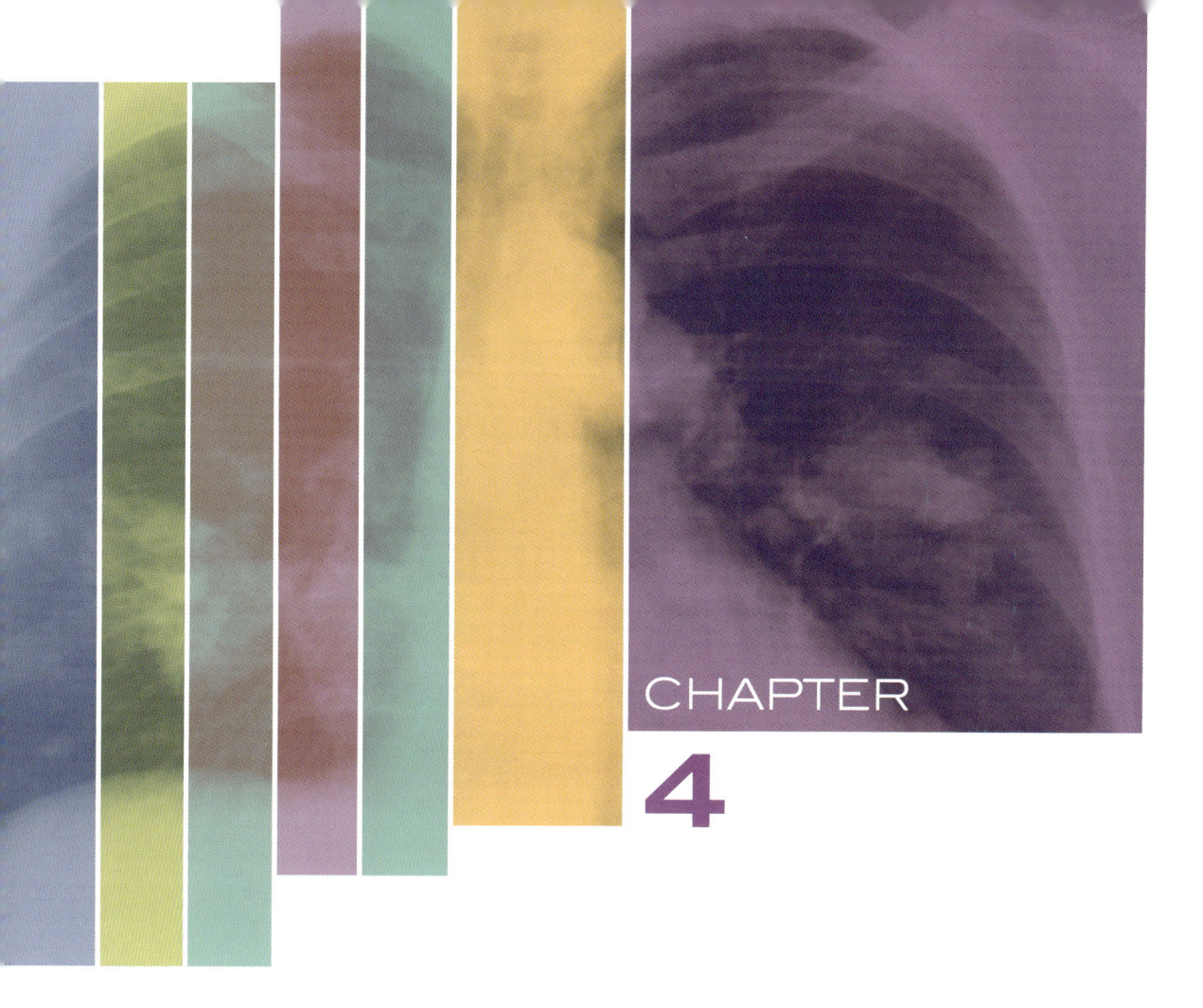

SYMPTOMS, DIAGNOSIS, AND ADVANCED STAGES

Warning signs differ, depending on whether the leukemia is acute or chronic. Leukemia symptoms are generally related to what is happening in the bone marrow, when bad white blood cells take over the bone marrow and other organs, there is less room for normal white and red blood cells and platelets. Symptoms produced by bad white blood cells include bone pain, no appetite, weight loss, night sweats, frequent infections, swollen lymph nodes, and an enlarged liver or spleen. Symptoms caused by low red blood cells include headaches, tiredness, and paleness. Symptoms due to low platelets include easy bruising and bleeding.

Leukemia can be difficult to diagnose, in part because early symptoms are the same as for many other diseases and conditions. Headaches and fatigue, for example, can indicate merely stress, a poor diet—or leukemia.

With chronic (slow-developing) leukemias, some victims don't exhibit any of the typical symptoms. They may live for years not realizing that they have a dangerous disease. They may learn about it accidentally during a routine medical checkup. A simple blood test might reveal a worrisome imbalance in the blood count.

For teenagers, making a diagnosis of leukemia might be particularly difficult. As their bodies mature, many teens are not comfortable discussing physical symptoms with adults. When they do voice a complaint, a parent may think the matter is insignificant—just another trait of being a teenager. For instance, one early symptom of leukemia is frequent fatigue. To a parent, as well as to the young person, this might be considered a predictable consequence of late-night cramming for a test or socializing.

DIAGNOSIS: A DIFFICULT CHALLENGE

A major problem in diagnosing leukemia is that early symptoms may be subtle or do not point just to leukemia. Patients can be easily misdiagnosed because the same symptoms occur with dozens of less dangerous diseases and conditions. For instance, fatigue, loss of appetite, and night sweats may be associated with flulike illnesses or mononucleosis (mono). Headache and tiredness can occur from iron-deficiency anemia (low levels of red blood cells due to a lack of iron intake) or stress. A blood test and physical exam are necessary to determine if the cause of such symptoms is far more serious.

Although leukemia is not common, it is important to pay attention to worrisome symptoms. If they persist more than a few days or weeks, a doctor should be consulted. Ignoring serious health problems is not likely to make them go away.

Treatment Begins

If leukemia is diagnosed, doctors decide on the best course of treatment. Some treatments happen in the clinic (where patients come and go in the same day), while other treatments require being admitted to a hospital. Most leukemia is treated with a combination of chemotherapy medicines designed to attack the bad cells from many different angles. Some patients also require moderate doses of radiation therapy, depending on the type of leukemia. Some patients with ALL, AML, or CML also require a bone marrow transplant.

Many blood tests will be conducted during and after treatment to monitor the progress of the disease and the effects of treatment. Some tests will check the function of the body's organs, such as the liver and kidneys. Other tests will monitor the blood counts and determine if a person needs a blood transfusion. Bone marrow tests and spinal taps may also be performed for patients with some types of leukemias. Patients sometimes need special imaging studies, such as ultrasound of the heart (echocardiogram), to ensure that the body's organs are working properly during treatment.

It takes a whole team of people to take care of patients with cancers such as leukemia. The doctors who treat patients with leukemia and direct their therapy are known as hematologists, oncologists, or hematologist-oncologists (depending on their training). Other doctors specialize in bone marrow transplants. Doctors called pathologists help make the initial diagnosis of leukemia by looking at blood and bone marrow under a microscope and performing specialized tests. If indicated, radiation oncologists—doctors who specialize in radiation therapy—may be involved. Surgeons may help place special catheters into the veins through which to give chemotherapy. Nurses take blood samples and give medicines, as well as provide other daily care. Pharmacists help with medicines.

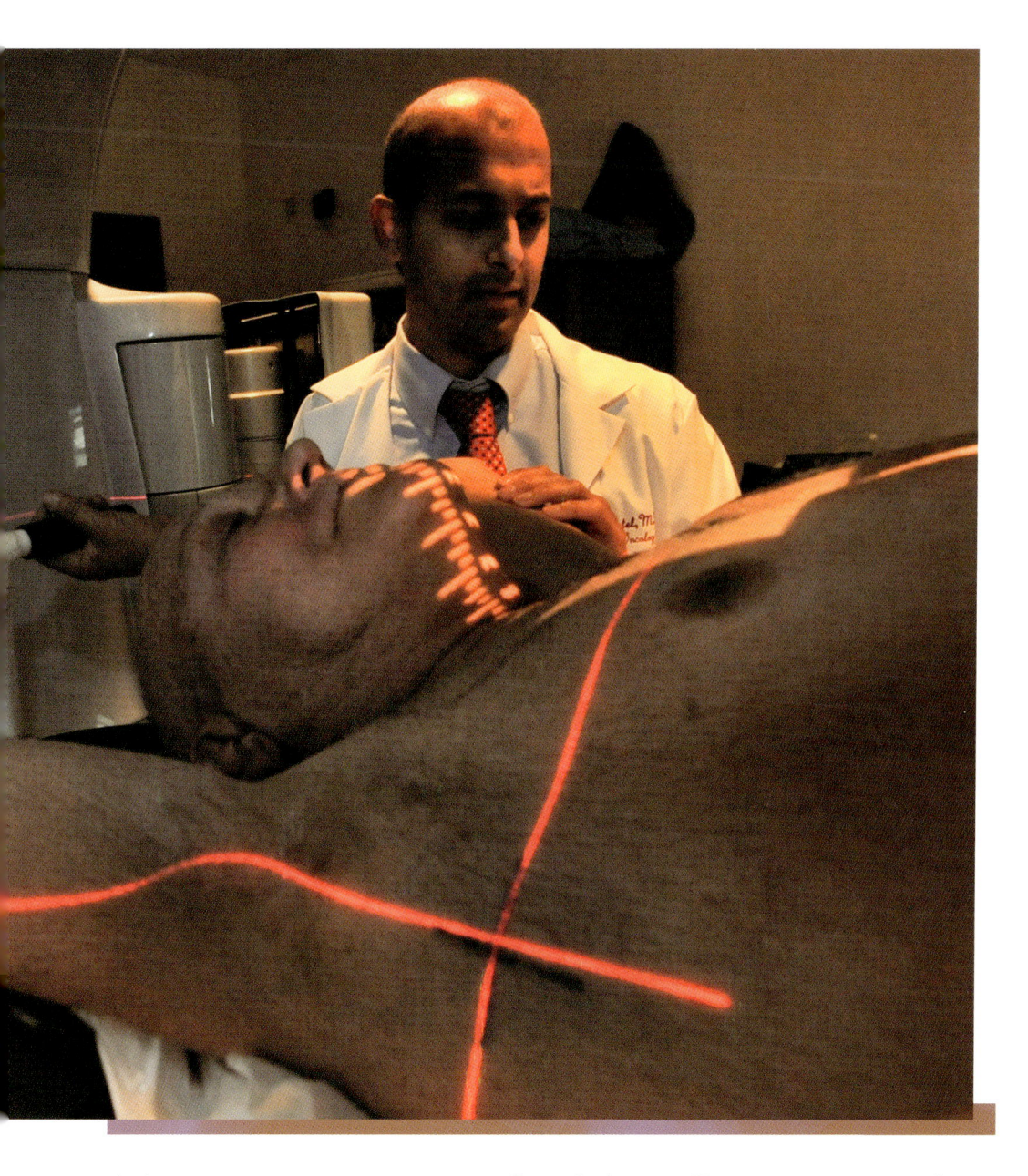

A doctor prepares a cancer patient for radiotherapy. Treatments are typically performed at hospitals or doctors' clinics.

Social workers provide support and help with life's disruptions. For pediatric patients, child life specialists help with play therapy and coping strategies.

Treatment Can Be Dangerous

Chemotherapy medicines are strong agents designed to attack cancer cells such as leukemia. These medicines are not without potential side effects, though, which doctors must always discuss with their patients. For example, some chemotherapies kill good white blood cells, too. This makes patients more susceptible to infections. Other chemotherapies for leukemia can have long-lasting effects on the heart, pancreas, kidneys, brain, or bones. Unfortunately, leukemias may be cured with good therapies, but the consequences of such treatments may be pretty undesirable.

The side effects of chemotherapy are not the only hazards. Having a special catheter makes people more likely to develop infections. A bone marrow transplant is particularly dangerous because it temporarily wipes out the patient's immune system. This leads to increased infection risk and other effects on the body's organs. Some transplants are even riskier because of the increased chance of graft-versus-host disease (GVHD). This results when the recipient's body rejects the transplanted bone marrow. GVHD can affect many of the body's organs, including the skin, liver, lungs, and intestines.

Side Effects of Treatment

Leukemia cannot be treated without unpleasant potential side effects. General side effects of chemotherapy include fatigue, nausea and vomiting, hair loss, risk of infection, need for blood transfusions, and problems with later fertility. Each medication also has individual side effects. For instance, steroids—a big component of leukemia treatment—can cause unpleasant weight gain, bloating, sleep problems, and grouchiness.

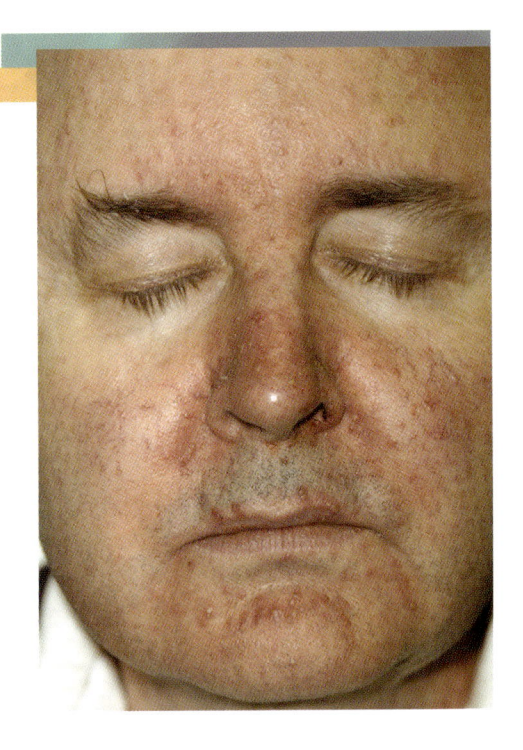

Chemicals used to treat cancer patients can produce unpleasant side effects. In this case, the facial skin rash was caused by a drug called Tarceva.

These side effects are especially devastating to teenagers. They are at a period in life when physical appearance is particularly important.

Some side effects can affect the patient permanently. One example is weakness of the bones due to steroid treatment. In an extreme example, a patient diagnosed at age fifteen was successfully treated for leukemia, but she had to undergo nine bone-related operations by the age of twenty-two, including hip replacements. Because of her weakened frame, she could not drive.

Most patients with leukemia fortunately do not require radiation treatment. Treatment many decades ago included the routine use of radiation for children with leukemia, which later was found to lead to significant learning problems. For most patients, radiation to the brain and spine has been replaced with chemotherapy given through the spinal fluid.

Radiation treatment is usually administered five days a week for a month or longer. Treatment itself does not hurt, although it can cause fatigue and skin irritation in some patients.

Advanced Stages of Leukemia

Thousands of patients conquer their leukemias every year. Some can resume basically normal lifestyles after fairly short-term treatment. For many others, treatment is grueling and long. Unfortunately, some patients will not survive their treatments, or their leukemias will relapse (come back) and be harder to treat. For such patients, the leukemia cells will eventually take over the body's vital organs and cause them to shut down if further treatment is not successful. Patients experience a progressive loss of physical and mental control. Chemotherapy can be used to slow down this process, even if it is not likely to cure the leukemia.

Some patients with incurable leukemia decide not to get any more treatment so that they can enjoy life without taking too many medicines or being stuck in the hospital. Others try new, experimental treatments or enroll in clinical trials to help researchers develop new medicines for people with leukemia.

TEN GREAT QUESTIONS TO ASK YOUR DOCTOR

1. Is leukemia a common form of cancer?

2. Are certain people more at risk for developing particular types of leukemia?

3. What causes leukemia? Are there precautions I should take or habits I should lose to prevent getting leukemia?

4. Is leukemia more common in certain geographic areas or among certain people?

5. What are the odds of surviving leukemia?

6. Can leukemia be cured permanently?

7. Besides chemotherapy, medications, and possibly radiation, are there other ways to treat leukemia? Is surgery an option?

8. What are the first symptoms of leukemia?

9. Is it possible to live a normal life—continue school, hold a job, raise a family—while battling leukemia?

10. What areas of research hold the greatest promise for developing leukemia cures and treatments?

CHAPTER 5

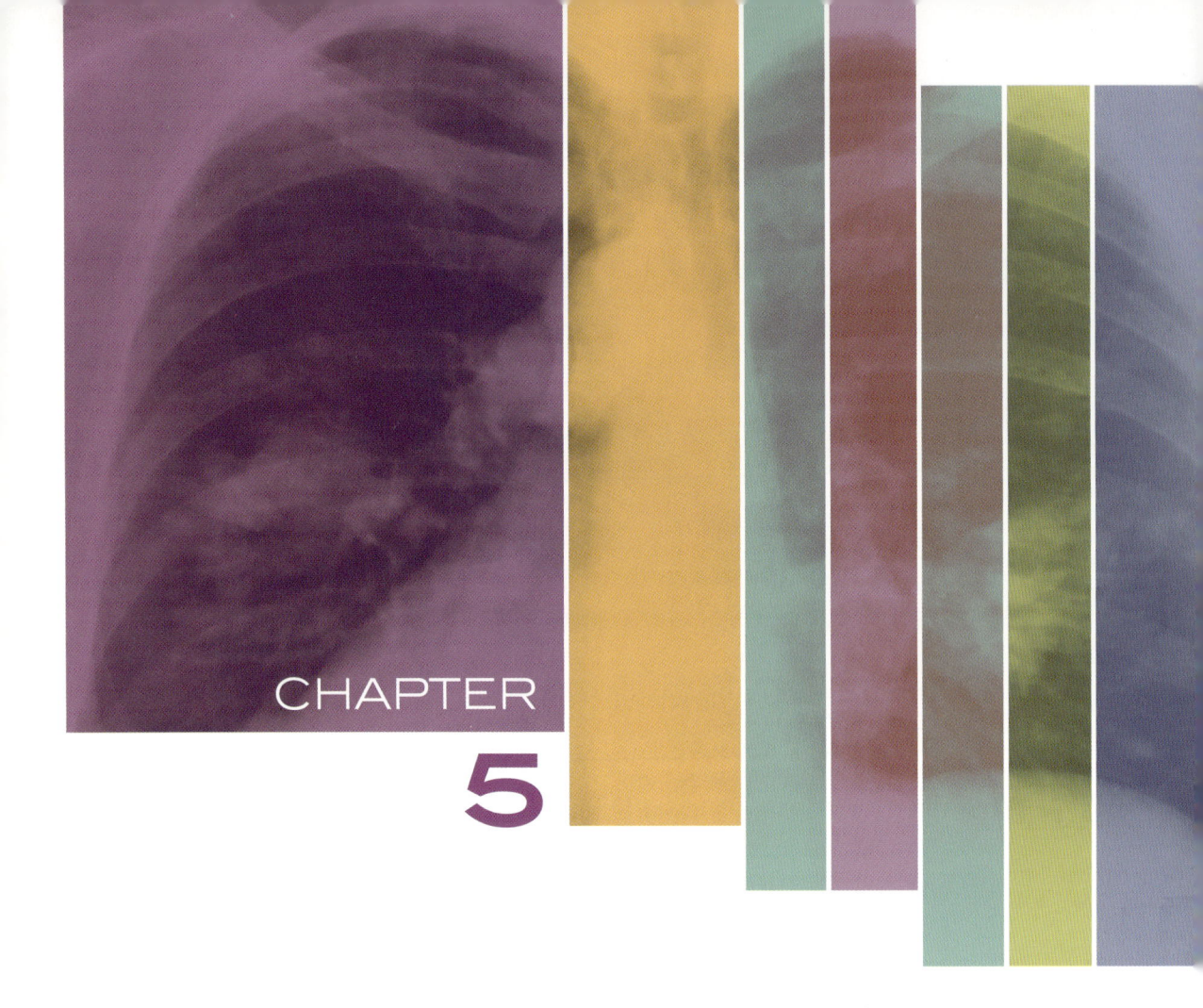

TREATING AND COPING WITH THE DISEASE

Leukemia is what doctors call "systemic." That means it doesn't affect just one part of the body. It affects entire systems (blood vessels, lymph nodes, and other organs). Because of that, leukemia has to be treated with agents that affect the whole body.

Chemotherapy is the most common treatment of leukemia. Different medicines are prescribed for different types of leukemia. In most cases, a combination of chemicals is given to the patient in order to attack the leukemia cells by different strategies. Doctors loosely call this multidrug solution a "chemo cocktail."

Treatments may last several months to several years, depending on the type of leukemia. Doctors determine the lowest dosages of medications that will keep the disease under control with the least severe side effects.

Stem cell (bone marrow) transplants have proved effective for certain patients, although transplants are not without risk.

Chemotherapy: New Agents

Many medications are commonly used in leukemia treatment. Most are systemic chemotherapies that attack rapidly dividing leukemia cells. They also affect healthy cells in the body, which causes undesirable side effects.

There has been great interest in targeted therapies, or medicines that recognize and attack only bad cancer cells. An example of a targeted therapy used for CML and some rare forms of ALL is imatinib, which attacks the bad Philadelphia chromosomes within leukemia cells. (Recall that the Philadelphia chromosome forms by two normal chromosomes breaking down and swapping pieces.) Other targeted therapies currently used for some leukemias include dasatinib and nilotinib.

Another interesting medicine used to treat one type of AML called acute promyelocytic leukemia is all-trans retinoic acid (ATRA). This chemotherapy does not actually kill the immature leukemia cell but causes it to develop into a more mature, less harmful cell.

Some chemotherapies are administered directly into the bloodstream by placing an IV into a vein. For children and patients whose veins are in poor condition, a device called a catheter can be surgically inserted into a larger vein, usually in the chest or upper arm. Through it, medicine can be administered regularly. Blood transfusions can be given, and blood draws can be obtained for lab testing. The major advantage of a central catheter is that the patient doesn't have to be pricked with a syringe each time.

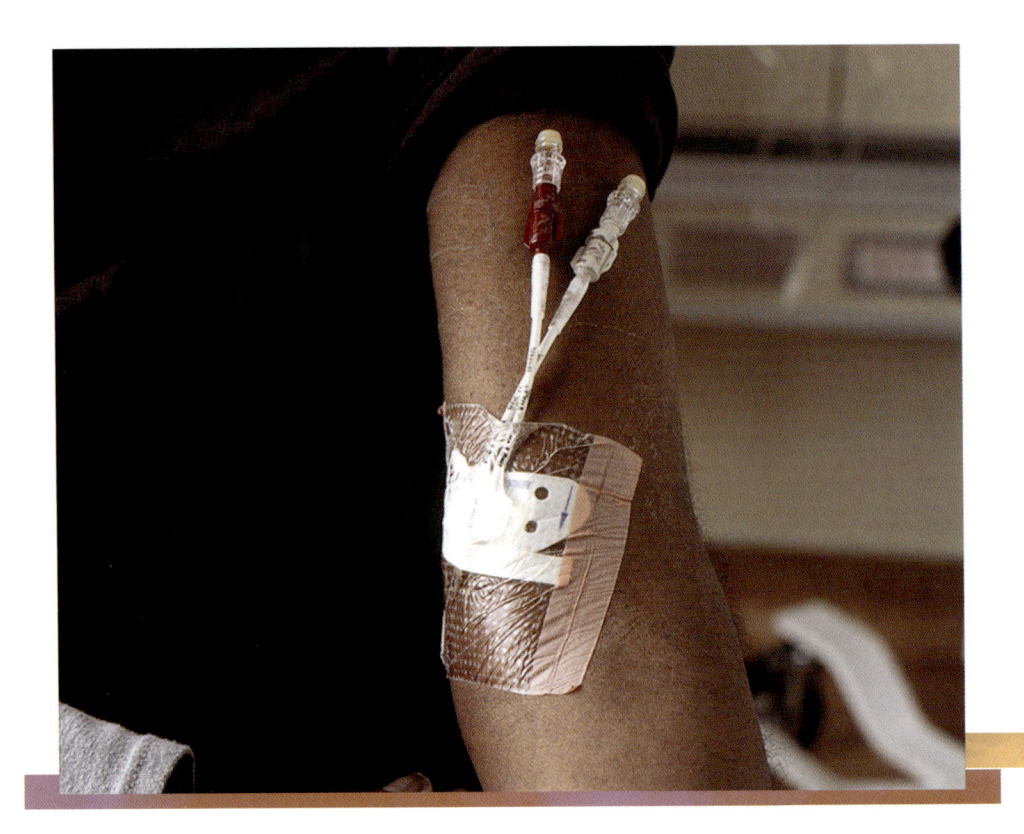

A catheter is a device through which chemotherapy can be administered without the need for repeated insertions of a syringe. It also simplifies the drawing of blood samples.

Bone Marrow Transplants

The purpose of a transplant is to replace damaged bone marrow with healthy marrow. In this process, bone marrow is obtained from a healthy donor and given to the patient. The donor can be a family member or an unrelated person, but it is important to have as good a match as possible. This means certain genetic characteristics of the donor's and recipient's bone marrow should be as similar as possible.

WHERE ARE PATIENTS TREATED?

Adults are usually treated for their leukemias at hospitals known as cancer centers. Children and teens are most often treated at specialized pediatric hospital cancer centers. The type of leukemia and the stage of treatment dictate whether a patient can be treated in the outpatient clinic or office or whether he or she has to be admitted to the hospital to receive the chemotherapy.

Some chemotherapy is in pill form and can be taken at home. Frequent blood tests during the treatment period reveal if the medicine is not being taken as prescribed.

What happens with a bone marrow transplant? There are actually three sources of stem cells (cells that can develop into all of the blood-forming cells) that can be given for a transplant. In a traditional transplant, bone marrow is obtained from the donor through a process called a harvest. After giving pain medicine (or placing the person under general anesthesia), a doctor inserts a hollow needle into the back of the donor's hips and aspirates out some of the liquid bone marrow. This bone marrow is then filtered and prepared in a laboratory. Meanwhile, the recipient is given large doses of chemotherapy to get rid of bad bone marrow (the leukemia) and make room for new, healthy stem cells. Over a few weeks, the healthy cells repopulate the bone marrow and develop into all of the different blood cells.

Other sources of stem cells that can be transplanted include umbilical cord blood (the blood that comes from the cord connecting a fetus to its placenta) and peripheral blood stem cell collection (stem cells that circulate in the bloodstream and can be collected through a special IV instead of a bone marrow harvest).

E. Donnall Thomas performed the first successful bone marrow transplant for a leukemia patient in 1957 in Seattle, Washington. (Although temporarily cured, the patient died after the leukemia returned six months later.) For years afterward, it was considered too risky for most patients. Only those near death, having no other hope, were given transplants. Although still a very serious procedure, bone marrow transplants have cured many people of their leukemias.

Radiation and Surgery

There is little role for surgery in the management of patients with leukemia. Again, this is because the disease is systemic. Surgery is generally used to remove a disease that affects a particular part of the body, such as a bone cancer or thyroid cancer. Some patients with leukemia do require central catheters to be placed surgically so that they can receive their chemotherapy.

Radiation is used much less commonly for leukemia patients than in the past. It is now mostly used for certain high-risk types of leukemia, and it is used at much lower doses than before. Radiation can be part of the preparation of a leukemia patient for a bone marrow transplant to get rid of the diseased bone marrow.

Immunotherapy

Some patients with leukemia can also be treated with a new strategy called immunotherapy. This approach to cancer treatment uses special proteins that target leukemia cells and mark them for destruction. These cancer-killing agents are injected by needle into the patient's bloodstream. Medical scientists believe this can be done without damaging healthy blood cells.

TREATING AND COPING WITH THE DISEASE   45

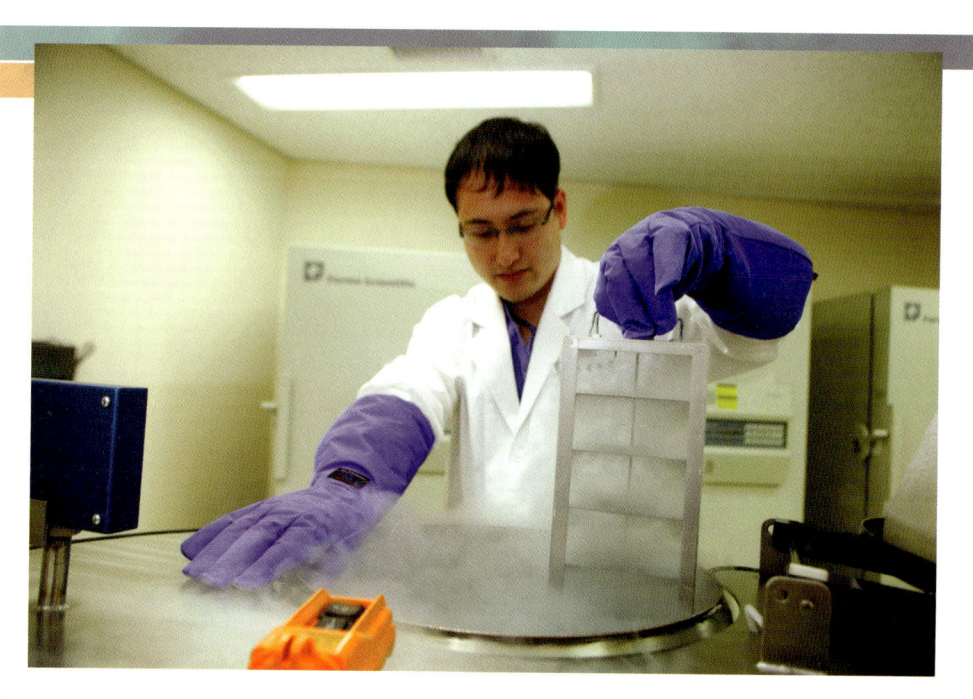

Researchers constantly seek new and improved treatments for cancer. This research center focuses on immunotherapy, bone marrow transplants, genetic treatment, and biotherapy.

COPING AND HOPING

Leukemia treatment complicates the patient's life physically, emotionally, and mentally. Patients with leukemia must deal with two hardships: the disease itself and the troublesome effects of treatment. The hope of all leukemia patients is that treatment will send the disease into remission. In remission, no trace of it can be detected. But the term can be deceptive because the illness unfortunately can return (relapse). In cases of acute lymphocytic leukemia, the American Cancer Society explains: "In general, about 80 percent to 90 percent of adults will have complete remissions after treatment. That means leukemia cells can no longer be seen in their bone marrow. But in about half of these patients the cancer will come back (relapse), so the overall cure rate is around 30 percent to 40 percent." For children with ALL, though, only about 15 to 20 percent relapse.

Nonetheless, many forms of leukemia are curable with proper treatment. Many patients after treatment enjoy long, normal lives with no recurrences. Patients must be monitored very closely during and after treatment to ensure that the leukemia is truly gone, however. Authors Edward D. Ball and Alex Kagan, in *100 Questions & Answers About Leukemia*, point out, "For all forms of leukemia, there is always a slight chance of relapse." *The Mayo Clinic Family Health Book*, describing CML, observes, "For most people, it's not possible to eliminate all diseased blood cells, but treatment can help achieve a long-term remission."

Regular medical checkups are thus essential for all leukemia patients.

CHAPTER 6

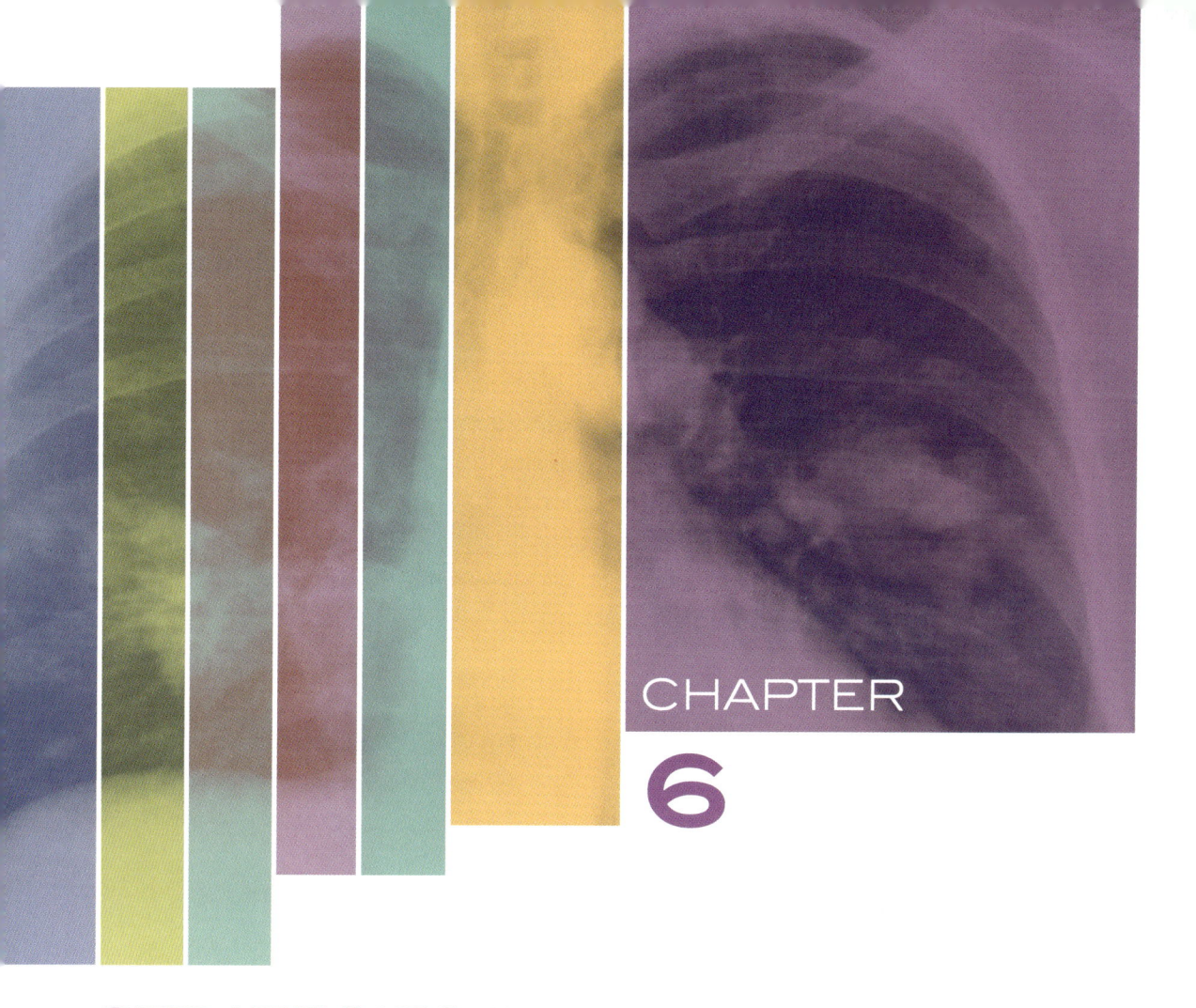

STRATEGIES IN LEUKEMIA RESEARCH

Scientists are trying to combat leukemia in different ways. The goal is to attack the abnormal proteins that allow leukemia cells to grow uncontrollably. Doctors prescribe different drugs for patients with different forms of leukemia.

GETTING NEW MEDICINES TO PATIENTS

The reason it takes so long to develop chemotherapy medications is that these drugs require extensive research. When scientists believe they may have found a chemical or chemical combination that can fight leukemia, they must prove the substance is effective at attacking leukemia cells and is safe to give to people. Only about one in ten thousand drugs that are studied in the lab ever make it to patients.

The U.S. Food and Drug Administration (FDA) is the government agency that oversees drug testing. It decides when a new medication is ready for doctors to prescribe to their patients. Mainly, FDA decisions are based on the results of extensive and well-regulated clinical trial testing. Patients are monitored very closely during and after their involvement in a clinical trial.

Clinical Trials

Drug companies that experiment with new medicines must conduct lengthy (and expensive) clinical testing. Some trial medications are completely new. Others have proved effective against certain diseases and are being tried in new ways against other diseases.

New drugs are usually first studied in cells in the lab. The next step is to administer the drug to an animal, such as a mouse, to see if it is effective and well tolerated. If the positive effects are promising and ill effects are minor, testing can later occur in human patients. New medicines are never tried on humans until they have been tested at great length in pre-clinical trials. Human patients must meet strict conditions, or doctors will not accept them into a trial program

Human drug testing is conducted in several phases, with increasing numbers of participating patients. In Phase I clinical trials, researchers want to make sure that the drug is safe. They also want to determine the most effective dosage to give patients. In Phase II trials, they administer the set dosage to a larger group of participants. Results are closely monitored and compared among the individuals. In Phase III trials, researchers expand their studies. They want to know, for example,

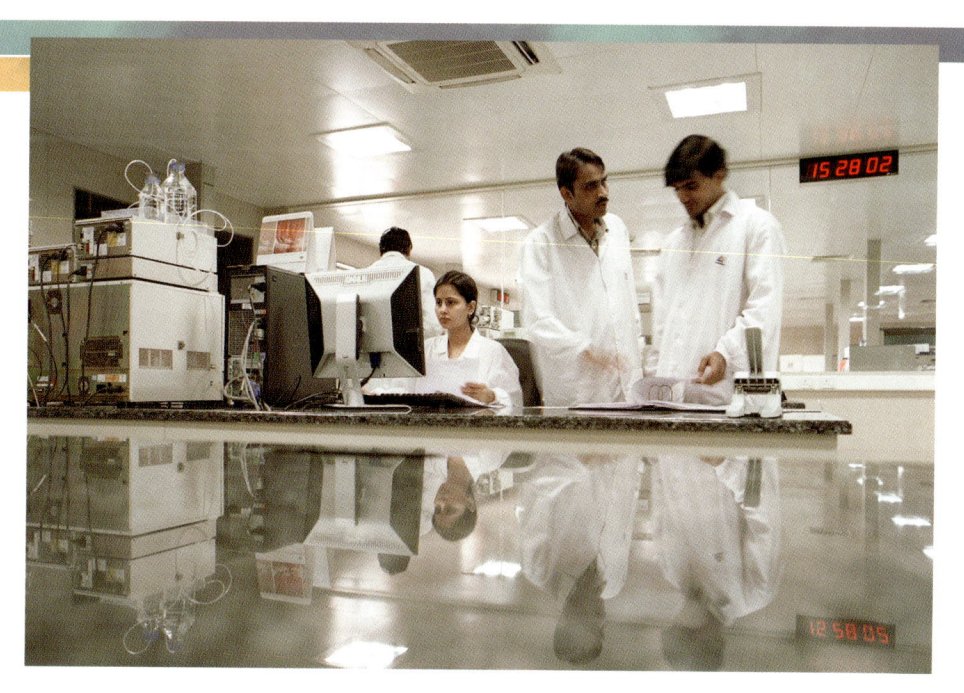

Lab technicians for a chemical company employ the latest high-technology tools in performing drug trials. Clinical testing is carefully monitored over a long period of time.

whether the new drug might be more effective if combined with another drug.

Most participants in Phase I and II trials are patients whose disease has relapsed or is refractory. (Refractory cancers are those that are particularly resistant to treatment.) In their cases, no existing treatments have been effective. The majority of tests are Phase III trials. By this stage, the experimental drug or drug combination has already been analyzed for a long time.

Clinical tests can take many years. Trial patients may withdraw from a study at any time, or they may be removed if doctors detect negative effects.

WHO TAKES PART IN CLINICAL TRIALS?

Many participants in new drug testing are patients with late stages of a disease. They hope that a new treatment may be effective for them, or they hope to help other patients in the future have better therapies. A great incentive to participate in a trial is that this is the cutting edge of medical progress. Patients in trial programs are exposed to some of the most promising cures under development.

Patients of different ages who are in different stages of a disease may be selected to take part in a clinical trial. They are pretested to ensure maximum safety. Doctors need to know, for example, whether they have physical conditions other than cancer that might be complicated by the treatment.

The National Cancer Institute (http://www.cancer.gov) provides information about clinical trial programs throughout the United States.

Some experimental drugs that show promise in helping people with dire illnesses are given accelerated development/review status. In effect, the FDA puts them on a fast track toward approval. Patients who are terminally ill may be enrolled in such trials to receive medications that have not been approved yet for the general public. These patients reason, "I am dying, and no other medicines are available to help me. What do I have to lose by trying this experimental drug?" Experimental drugs for deadly diseases such as cancer and AIDS are the ones most likely to be granted fast-track status. Great treatment advances have been made because of people who have participated in clinical trials.

Even when a new drug is approved, after years of clinical tests, problems with it can arise. A drug can affect one patient differently from another—and it may have nothing to do with the patient's disease. In some cases, it is decades before patients begin to realize bad (even fatal) effects. News reports often tell of drugs that are suddenly banned from the market—drugs that doctors have prescribed confidently for a long time.

Cancer Fights Back

The challenge of developing new drugs to kill cancer cells is partly a game of medical cat-and-mouse. Some cancer cells fight back. They can evade chemotherapy by mutating, or changing their genetic material. They can thereby make themselves immune to the drug. Researchers constantly strive to develop new drugs that are able to deal more effectively with disease mutations.

Because of that, doctors for years have been prescribing medicinal cocktails—combinations of drugs. Doctors hope that between them, they will get rid of all the bad cells. Finding new, more effective cocktails is another strategy in leukemia research.

Scientists and physicians also hope to develop medications that will kill leukemia cells but cause fewer unpleasant side effects on healthy cells.

Can Special Diets and Vitamin Supplements Help?

There is no diet that will cure a person of leukemia. It is important, however, for patients with leukemia to eat healthfully and drink enough fluids. It can be tough to eat properly when a person is nauseated from chemotherapy or doesn't have much energy. A nutritionist (a person skilled in the knowledge of healthy, balanced diets) can be an important resource for cancer patients.

A nutritionist instructs a patient in the importance of portion sizes. A healthy diet helps stave off diseases and is vital, though difficult to maintain, for cancer patients.

As for diet supplements, many doctors do not advise patients to buy special vitamin tablets, capsules, or drinks. They consider them a waste of money. In some cases, large doses of certain vitamins can prevent a chemotherapy medicine from working properly. Patients should always consult a doctor before taking any vitamin, herb, or supplement. Some can be very dangerous, while others are OK in standard doses.

Reasons for Optimism

Efforts to conquer leukemia have been very encouraging. For example, the overall survival rate for children with ALL in the 1960s was less than

Researchers for the National Cancer Institute study blood and tissue samples. Leukemia research is carried out by government agencies as well as private and academic institutions.

10 percent. Now, cure rates for children are higher than 85 percent. Similarly, adults with ALL thirty years ago had only a 38 percent likelihood of surviving to five years after therapy. Their long-term survival rate is now 65 percent. Thanks to modern medications such as imatinib and dasatinib, patients with other forms of leukemia also have greater hope today than ever before.

As with other types of cancer, scientific and medical research continues in earnest. The National Institutes of Health and various other government and private organizations fund leukemia research and are essential to advancing new treatments. The research will end only when ways are found to cure each disease—or prevent it.

GLOSSARY

anemia A blood condition characterized by a low count of red blood cells.
biopsy Removal of a small portion of skin or other tissue for the purpose of medical testing.
bone marrow Soft substance in the hollow of bones where blood is produced.
carbon dioxide A colorless, odorless gas.
cell The smallest independent part of an animal or plant.
cellular pathology The study of changes caused by diseased cells.
chemotherapy The use of chemicals to treat diseases.
chromosome A gene-carrying structure within a cell.
clinical trial Testing of an experimental medicine.
DNA The main part of a chromosome.
donor An individual who volunteers to contribute a physical component to a needy patient.
electromagnetic field Combination of electrical and magnetic forces.
gene The basic physical structure that transmits character traits to offspring.

GLOSSARY

genetics Hereditary characteristics.
hematologist A doctor who specializes in blood diseases.
lymph node A part of the body that filters infectious microorganisms.
lymphatic system The network that moves healthy elements to the bloodstream and removes unhealthy elements.
lymphoma Form of cancer that originates in the lymphatic system.
mononucleosis A viral syndrome characterized by fatigue, high white blood cell counts, and an enlarged spleen.
mutate To change from one form to another.
oncologist A doctor who treats cancer.
platelet A specialized blood cell that helps injured blood vessels to clot.
protein A molecule that allows proper functioning of cells.
radioactivity The emission of high-energy particles from certain substances.
relapse The recurrence of cancer after a period of remission.
remission A period during which symptoms of a cancer are partly or completely gone.
spleen Organ in the upper-left abdomen that filters the blood.
syringe Medical device used to withdraw blood or inject something into the bloodstream.
virologist A scientist who studies viruses and the diseases they can produce.

FOR MORE INFORMATION

American Cancer Society
250 Williams Street NW
Atlanta, GA 30303
(800) 227-2345
Web site: http://www.cancer.org
A nationwide, community-based, voluntary health organization, the American Cancer Society is dedicated to preventing cancer and diminishing patients' suffering.

Canadian Cancer Society
Suite 200, 10 Alcorn Avenue
Toronto, ON M4V 3B1
Canada
(416) 961-7223
Web site: http://www.cancer.ca
This is a community-based national network that is devoted to eradicating cancer and improving the quality of life of cancer patients.

Centers for Disease Control and Prevention (CDC)
1600 Clifton Road
Atlanta, GA 30333
(800) 232-4636
Web site: http://www.cdc.gov
The federal government's CDC maintains an updated online communication resource for all disease-related matters.

CureSearch
Children's Oncology Group
Research Operations Center
440 East Huntington Drive, Suite 400
Arcadia, CA 91006-3776
(800) 458-6223
Web site: http://www.curesearch.org/for_parents_and_families
CureSearch provides information about clinical trials for pediatric oncology patients.

Lance Armstrong Foundation
2201 E. Sixth Street
Austin, TX 78702
(877) 236-8820
Web site: http://www.laf.org
This nonprofit cancer support group was founded by world-champion cyclist Lance Armstrong, who is a cancer survivor.

Leukemia & Lymphoma Society
1311 Mamaroneck Avenue, Suite 310
White Plains, NY 10605
(800) 955-4572

Web site: http://www.leukemia.org
The Leukemia & Lymphoma Society is "the world's largest voluntary health agency dedicated to blood cancer."

Leukemia Research Foundation
3220 Lake Avenue, Suite 202
Wilmette, IL 60091
(847) 424-0600
Web site: http://www.leukemia-research.org
This organization is devoted to conquering leukemia, lymphoma, and myelodysplastic syndromes through research and improving patients' quality of life.

National Cancer Institute (NCI)
6116 Executive Boulevard, Room 3036A
Bethesda, MD 20892-8322
(800) 422-6237
Web site: http://www.cancer.gov
Created by the U.S. Congress in 1937, the NCI is considered the world's leading cancer research organization.

WEB SITES

Due to the changing nature of Internet links, Rosen Publishing has developed an online list of Web sites related to the subject of this book. This site is updated regularly. Please use this link to access the list:

http://www.rosenlinks.com/cms/leuk

FOR FURTHER READING

Bozzone, Donna M. *Causes of Cancer* (The Biology of Cancer). New York, NY: Chelsea House Publishers, 2007.

Bozzone, Donna M. *Leukemia* (The Biology of Cancer). New York, NY: Chelsea House/Infobase Publishing, 2009.

Chilman-Blair, Kim. *What's Up with Richard? Medikidz Explain Leukemia* (Medikidz Explain [Cancer XYZ]). Atlanta, GA: American Cancer Society, 2010.

Harmon, Daniel E. *New Medicines: Issues of Approval, Access, and Product Safety* (Science and Society). New York, NY: Rosen Publishing, 2009.

Langwith, Jacqueline. *Leukemia* (Perspectives on Diseases & Disorders). Farmington Hills, MI: Greenhaven Press, 2009.

Lyons, Lyman. *Diagnosis and Treatment of Cancer* (The Biology of Cancer). New York, NY: Chelsea House Publishers, 2007.

Mareck, Amy M. *Fighting for My Life: Growing Up with Cancer*. Minneapolis, MN: Fairview Press, 2007.

Owens, Jim. *The Survivorship Net: A Parable for the Family, Friends, and Caregivers of People with Cancer*. Atlanta, GA: American Cancer Society, 2010.

BIBLIOGRAPHY

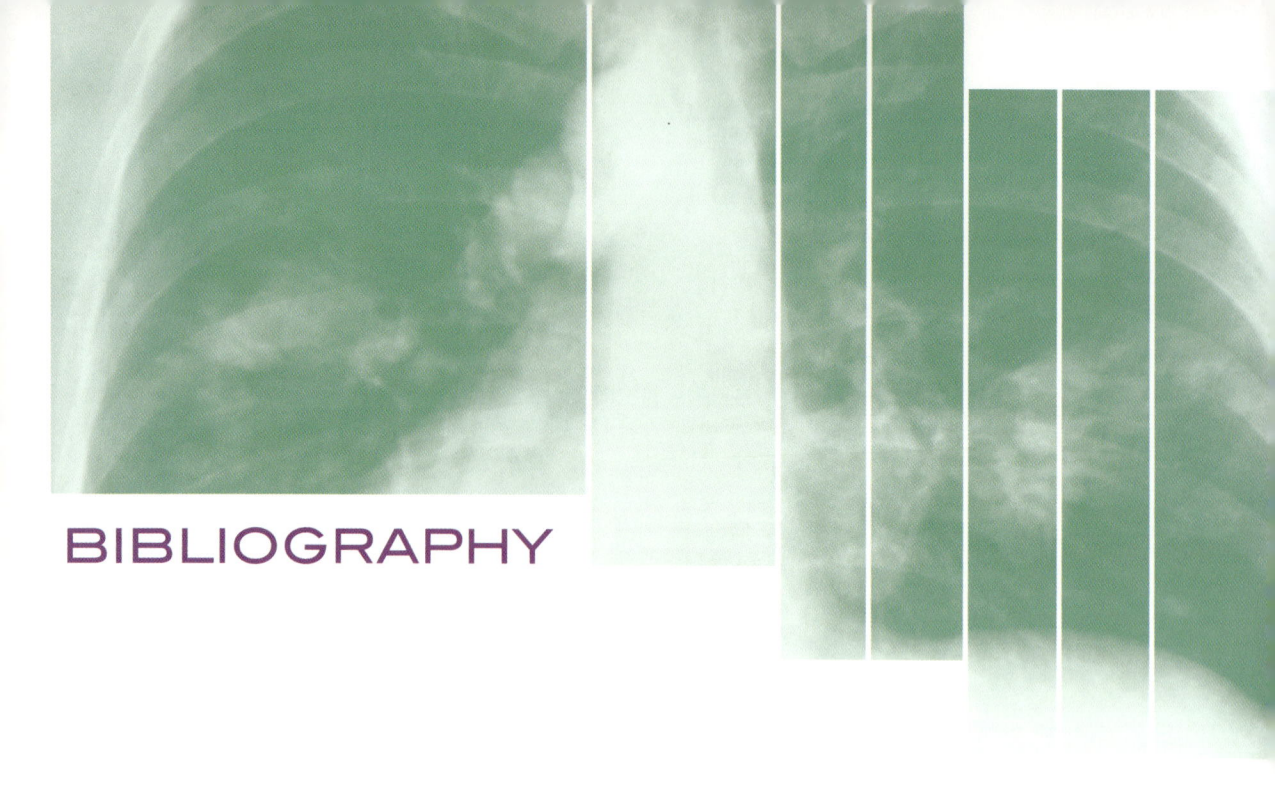

Ball, Edward D., and Alex Kagan. *100 Questions & Answers About Leukemia*. 2nd ed. Sudbury, MA: Jones and Bartlett Publishers, 2008.

Bellenir, Karen, ed. *Cancer Sourcebook* (Health Reference Series). 5th ed. Detroit, MI: Omnigraphics, 2007.

Bellenir, Karen, ed. *Cancer Survivorship Sourcebook* (Health Reference Series). Detroit, MI: Omnigraphics, 2007.

Canadian Cancer Society. "What Is Leukemia?" Retrieved March 2010 (http://www.cancer.ca/Canada-wide/About%20cancer/Types%20of%20cancer/What%20is%20leukemia.aspx).

Cleveland Clinic. "Coping with Bone Marrow Transplantation." Retrieved April 5, 2010 (http://my.clevelandclinic.org/services/bone_marrow_transplantation/hic_coping_with_bone_marrow_transplantation.aspx).

Healy, Bernadine. *Living Time: Faith and Facts to Transform Your Cancer Journey*. New York, NY: Bantam Dell, 2007.

Kushi, Michio, and Alex Jack. *The Cancer Prevention Diet: The Macrobiotic Approach to Preventing and Relieving Cancer*, 25th Anniversary Edition. New York, NY: St. Martin's Griffin, 2009.

Leukemia & Lymphoma Society. "Facts & Statistics." Retrieved March 2010 (http://www.leukemia-lymphoma.org/all_page.adp?item_id=12486).

Leukemia & Lymphoma Society. "Leukemia Facts & Statistics." Retrieved March 2010 (http://www.lls.org//all_page?item_id=9346&gclid=CIzFq72n8qACFZVY2godKir5Xg).

Litin, Scott C., ed. *The Mayo Clinic Family Health Book*. 4th ed. Rochester, MN: Mayo Clinic/Time, Inc., 2009.

MedicineNet.com. "Definition of Irradiation." Retrieved April 5, 2010 (http://www.medterms.com/script/main/art.asp?articlekey=24435).

Morrow, Alina. "Leukemia Types & Stages." OmniMedicalSearch.com. Retrieved April 5, 2010 (http://www.omnimedicalsearch.com/conditions-diseases/leukemia-types.html).

National Bone Marrow Transplant Link. "Resource Guide for Bone Marrow/Stem Cell Transplant." Retrieved April 5, 2010 (http://www.nbmtlink.org/resources_support/rg/rg_costs.htm).

National Cancer Institute. "What You Need to Know About Leukemia." NIH Publication No. 08-3775. Retrieved March 2010 (http://www.cancer.gov/cancertopics/wyntk/leukemia).

Nordqvist, Christian. "What Is Leukemia? What Causes Leukemia?" *Medical News Today*, March 17, 2009. Retrieved April 6 2010 (http://www.medicalnewstoday.com/articles/142595.php).

Rabin, Roni Caryn. "In Cancer Fight, Teenagers Don't Fit In." *New York Times*, March 15, 2010. Retrieved March 16, 2010 (http://www.nytimes.com/2010/03/16/health/16canc.html).

Shannon, Joyce Brennfleck, ed. *Diet and Nutrition Sourcebook* (Health Reference Series). 3rd ed. Detroit, MI: Omnigraphics, 2006.

Teeley, Peter, and Philip Bashe. *The Completely Revised and Updated Cancer Survival Guide*. New York, NY: Broadway Books, 2005.

U.S. Food and Drug Administration. "Inside the Pyramid." Retrieved April 5, 2010 (http://www.mypyramid.gov/pyramid/index.html).

INDEX

A

acute lymphocytic leukemia (ALL), 14, 20, 21, 25, 27, 28, 33, 41, 45, 52–53
acute myelogenous leukemia (AML), 9, 13, 19, 20, 25, 27, 28, 33, 41
advancing age, and leukemia, 20
aspiration, 29–30

B

Bennett, John Hughes, 12
bone marrow, and leukemia, 8, 9, 11, 20–21, 23, 31, 42, 46
  testing of, 29–30, 34
bone marrow transplant, 25, 33, 36, 41, 42–44

C

cancer, causes of, 7–8, 11
catheters, 41, 44

chemicals, exposure to, and leukemia, 16, 18–19
chemotherapy, 18–19, 25, 33, 38, 40–41, 43, 51, 52
  development of new treatments, 47–48
  side effects of, 36–37, 41
chronic lymphocytic leukemia (CLL), 9, 21, 25, 28, 29
chronic myelogenous leukemia (CML), 25, 27, 28, 33, 41
clinical trials for new treatments, 48–51
Curie, Marie, 4, 6, 18

D

DNA, 6, 7, 27

E

electromagnetic fields, and leukemia, 19

G
Gallo, Robert, 18
genetics, and leukemia, 19–20

H
hairy cell leukemia, 29

I
immunotherapy, 44

J
Joliet-Curie, Irène, 4, 6, 18

L
leukemia
  about, 8–9, 13, 23
  advanced stages of, 38
  coping with, 45, 51–52
  diagnosing, 29–30, 32, 33, 34
  history of, 11–12
  myths and facts about, 15
  possible causes of, 16–22
  prevention of, 21–22
  questions to ask a doctor about, 39
  research into, 47–53
  statistics on, 4–6, 12–14, 15, 25, 28, 45–46, 52–53
  symptoms of, 9, 31–32, 33
  treatment of, 33–37, 38, 40–43, 45–46
  types of, 8–9, 23
Leukemia & Lymphoma Society, 4–6, 12, 22, 28
liquid cancer, 8, 12
lymphatic system, 8, 9, 11
lymphoma, 11

N
Neumann, Ernst, 11

P
Philadelphia chromosomes, 27, 41

R
radiation, 4, 16, 18
radiation therapy, 4, 33, 37, 44
  dangers of, 4, 18
red blood cells, 11, 20, 21, 31

S
side effects of leukemia treatment, 36–37
smoking, and leukemia, 19, 21
solid cancers, 8
spinal tap, 30, 34
stem cells, 41, 43–44
surgery, 34, 44

T
targeted therapies, 41
Thomas, E. Donnall, 44

U
U.S. Food and Drug Administration, 48, 50

V
Virchow, Rudolf, 11–12, 13
viruses, 16, 17–18

W
Waldeyer, Wilhelm, 11
white blood cells, 11, 36
  genetic changes in, 6, 9
  and leukemia, 4, 12, 20, 23, 25, 31

ABOUT THE AUTHOR

Daniel E. Harmon is the author of more than seventy books and thousands of magazine, newspaper, and newsletter articles. Previous works of his published by Rosen Publishing include *New Medicines: Issues of Approval, Access, and Product Safety*; *Obesity*; *Fish, Meat, and Poultry: Dangers in the Food Supply*; *Hallucinogens: The Dangers of Distorted Reality*; and *Frequently Asked Questions About Overscheduling and Stress*. Harmon lives in Spartanburg, South Carolina.

PHOTO CREDITS

Cover, pp. 1, 10 Science Photo Library/Custom Medical Stock Photo; cover (top), pp. 4–5 (bottom) Punchstock; back cover, border design, pp. 3, 7, 16, 17, 23, 31, 40, 42, 47, 53, 54, 56, 59, 60, 62 National Cancer Institute; book art LifeART image © 2010 Lippincott Williams & Wilkins. All rights reserved; pp. 5 (top), 12 Time Life Pictures/Mansell/Time Life Pictures/Getty Images; p. 8 Spike Walker/Stone/Getty Images; p. 14 Courtesy of the Tibbetts family; p. 19 George Doyle/Stockbyte/Thinkstock; p. 22 Comstock/Thinkstock; p. 24 (left) Custom Medical Stock Photo; p. 24 (right) Science VU/Visuals Unlimited; pp. 26–27 Kevin Laubacher/Taxi/Getty Images; p. 29 © Nucleus Medical Art, Inc./Phototake; p. 32 Stockbyte/Thinkstock; pp. 34–35 © AP Images; p. 37 Dr. P. Marazzi/Photo Researchers; p. 45 Medicimage LTD/Visuals Unlimited; p. 49 Stephan Elleringmann/laif/Redux; p. 52 © Yoav Levy/Phototake.

Designer: Evelyn Horovicz; Editor: Kathy Kuhtz Campbell; Photo Researcher: Marty Levick

DISCARD